# FROM BRITAIN TO SPAIN AND BACK AGAIN

*One English Family's Ultimately Uplifting Experience*

**SAM HAIGH**

*To Emma, for all her support and invaluable editing, and to Luke, for his good-humoured flexibility.*

# Introduction

This isn't a sad story, though we did have to make some tough decisions along the way. When I look back, the rose-tinted specs come in handy from time to time, but in writing this account I'll try to keep them off, so to speak, as the whole point of the exercise is to look back without either false jollity or whining regrets; in short, to tell it like it was, every step of the way. I mean, it would be easy enough to exaggerate or even make things up and turn it into one of those 'laugh out loud' books that make you smile half a dozen times, but that would be no use to either me or you, so I'll try to stick to the facts. In a nutshell, my wife Emma, our son Luke and I moved to Spain from England in 2007, moved back in 2011, and have made a go of it here since then.

Emma says that's too short for a book, and she's had more schooling than me, so I'll try to elaborate a little in the following chapters, which I hope will be entertaining and informative enough to make them worth reading. We're not the only people to give up on the 'Spanish Dream' and come back to Britain, not by a long chalk, and for us the process of returning and starting afresh has been at least as interesting and illuminating as going out there in the first place. I hope that our mostly positive experience will help to convince those who have a well-known Clash lyric in their heads – namely, 'Should I stay or should I go?' – that living in Spain isn't the be-all and end-all. It's not where you live, but how you live, as Emma said not long ago, and if we've learnt anything from our experience it's just how true that statement is.

If you're living in Spain and thinking of coming back, the title of the book will have caught your eye for that reason, but if you're thinking of moving *to* Spain I reckon it's worth a read too, especially if you're aged between thirty and fifty, aren't stinking rich, and have kids. It's not going to be a housing and paperwork horror story, by the way – there is plenty of reading matter about that side of things already – but more about our thoughts, feelings and reactions during our emotional and physical journeys.

Emma and I are as happy now as we were before embarking on our life-changing move, and I think Luke is too, though you never know with kids, especially adolescent ones. So, though there's a bit of doom and gloom at some points in our story, I've concluded that as long as you've got your health, another rainbow always appears sooner or later, and, as we all know, you need changeable weather to get decent rainbows.

# 1

I'm from Todmorden in West Yorkshire and it was a gloomy place to grow up in, though I was happy enough at the time, not knowing any different. It's still gloomy now, from a sunlight point of view, due to being in an extremely deep valley, but as it has experienced a sort of renaissance due to the overspill from the more arty and cosmopolitan Hebden Bridge, five miles up the valley, it's a lot more upbeat and diverse nowadays, though they haven't found a way to make the sun rise any higher in winter yet. Emma hails from Halifax, yet further along Calderdale, and we bought a large, and still fairly cheap, terraced house in my home town when we got married back in 1999.

I was thirty then, Emma a sprightly twenty-eight, and Luke just a glimmer in his parents' eyes that would be transformed in to flesh, bone and spirit in the spring of 2001. Emma had been teaching at a local primary school for a couple of years when we met in the Hare and Hounds pub around Christmastime, 1996. I had my beer goggles on at the time, though even through the alcoholic haze I knew I didn't need them to chat to this bright, pretty, petite brunette, and few weeks later we were 'going steady' according to my mum, and 'courting' according to my yet more antiquated Granddad. I too am a brunette, by the way, or maybe brunet's the right word, but I'm not exactly petit, weighing in at between thirteen and fourteen stone at various times between then and now.

Is that enough background detail? I ask myself at this point. For the purpose of this account I think it is, and there'll be time enough to write an eight volume autobiography when I'm older. It'll be one way of passing the time during our long English winters, but I'll come back to that topic later, and not in a negative way.

So, we set up home in not so sunny 'Tod' in the autumn of 1999 and, like most people, speculated on our likely fortunes once the new millennium got under way, assuming the world's logistics didn't grind to a halt and we all died of hunger, as Todmorden's 'Incredible Edible' vegetable growing project wasn't to be conceived for a few more years. Emma and I were fairly optimistic about our prospects, as she had a good, safe salary from her teaching, while I was earning even more from my building work, though that kind of work is more prone to fluctuations, as I was to find out in no uncertain terms a few years later, but I won't try to make you weep just yet.

Things were going great and when little Luke came along he was like the icing on the cake – though I doubt he'd appreciate being referred to in that way – and because we hadn't mortgaged ourselves to the hilt Emma was able to work just three days a week for the next six years. During that time, in fact, we saved quite a lot of money, as neither of us were spendthrifts and, let's face it, wages in Britain are pretty good in real terms, unless you live in the south-east and spend most of your income on your mortgage. More about this later too, as we met some expats in Spain from the Home Counties, and their having had an expensive house to sell before moving out sometimes proved to be a potentially double-edged sword, which more than one of them probably thought about impaling themselves on from time to time, but I digress, or get ahead of myself, or both.

So, there we were, getting on with our lives and enjoying each new stage in little Luke's growth and development, which Emma explained to me in technical terms, especially if things didn't seem to be going to plan, like when he started nursery and seemed clumsier than the other kids there. I'm not the first dad who's had high aspirations for his child, of course, but when I picked him up for the first time I'd rather hoped that he'd be the cock of the walk, which he wasn't; more like the lame duck, in fact, as he stumbled around as if he'd had a few pints at lunchtime.

"Don't worry, Sam," Emma said when I expressed my concern. "His motor skills are about average for his age."

"Average? I'd hoped for a bit more than that from our excellent genes."

"I hope you aren't going to be one of those dads who try to live their lives through their sons," she said pointedly, as it was at about that time that I'd eased off on the cycling, a sport in which I'd competed with moderate success since my late teens, but which had proved too time-consuming to combine with married and parental life.

"Course not, I just want him to hold his own."

"Good."

"And be the strongest, fastest and brightest kid in the nursery."

"Hmm, I thought as much. Just play with him and read to him and let him get on with his life. I've certainly got no plans to become a mother and nothing else."

Emma preferred walking to cycling, so I gradually moved over to her favoured form of locomotion rather than shooting off on my bike for hours on end. There are great walks from Todmorden, if you don't mind hills, but when you were born in a place, I guess you just take that sort of thing for granted. More about this later, and that, I promise, is the last time I'll use that phrase.

It was in the summer of 2005 when the seed of the idea of going to live in Spain was first planted. An older cycling friend of mine and his wife had come home to visit, about a year after their move to – you guessed it – Spain. Tim had retired from the police force at fifty and as his wife Sue didn't feel exactly heartbroken about packing in her office job, they'd sold up and bought a modest apartment down on the coast near Malaga. Tim and I weren't really close friends, but he'd called me to suggest a quick spin on the bikes and it was after climbing the horrendously steep hill out of Hebden Bridge – Mytholm Steeps, it's called – that we got our breath back and began to chat.

"How's life in Spain then, Tim?"

"Oh, it's great. It's a bit hot and touristy down there in summer, but the rest of the year it's fantastic. There are some great rides up from the coast and there are roads where you don't see a single car for ages."

"Right. What about when you're not cycling?" I asked, as though he was an inveterate pedaller, even he couldn't ride all day long.

"That's great too. I mean, I get out on the bike for two or three hours in the morning, then I have a swim in the sea in the afternoon."

"Followed by cocktails on the terrace?" I asked, already becoming a tad jealous.

"Ha, well, maybe a couple of beers, then a stroll along the front with Sue in the evening, watching the sun go down. It's grand, Sam. You ought to think about moving out there yourselves."

"Er, yes, it sounds great, but me and Emma are in a slightly different position to you two," I said, before pointing out the subtle differences in our lives as we began to coast down the long hill towards Burnley.

I'm sure I don't need to spell out those differences, but a couple in their mid-thirties with a small child aren't quite as footloose and fancy free as a retired couple, albeit a relatively youthful one, for at the time Tim was fifty-four and Sue a year older.

"And do you manage on your police pension?" I asked him.

"If we're careful, yes, but we do eat into our savings a bit now and then. The thing is, if we can get used to living on that, we're laughing, as Sue can take her private pension soon, and looking further ahead we'll have our state pensions too, touch wood," he said with a hint of self-satisfaction that I didn't find annoying, as it was clear that they'd really downsized in order to make ends meet, something that other people… well, you'll see soon enough.

"Well, me and Emma won't be able to do anything like that for at least twenty years," I said, preparing to change the subject, as it was making the damp day seem damper still.

"You could do it a lot sooner if you wanted to. They're crying out for builders over there, so you'd walk into a job, or, better still, you set up on your own and make a packet."

"What about Emma?"

"Oh, the locals are crying out for English teachers. She'd get a job in a language school no problem, or, better still, set up on her own and…"

"Make a packet?"

"Well, not as much as a builder, but you won't necessarily need that much money. I mean, houses are getting a bit dear just now, but you could always rent and see if you liked it. Look, we try to get by on about a thousand quid a month, though we don't go out that much, so you could make a do on, say, fifteen hundred. Ha, you could earn that working three days a week laying tiles."

"I don't especially like laying tiles," I said, as I considered myself more of an artisan builder than a mindless automaton.

"So you set up your own company. The Brits prefer British builders, as hardly any of them speak Spanish, so you'd have them queueing up."

"Then there's the language. How are you and Sue getting along with it?"

"Poco a poco."

"What?"

"Little by little. We're determined not to be total expats who can't even be arsed to speak Spanish in the shops and bars, so we're having classes. It's not so easy at our age, but your brains will still be more agile, and as for your lad, well, English kids start school there and by the end of the term they're chatting away like natives. Little sponges, they are."

"Hmm," I said, but it was one of my more pensive hmms.

We did less chatting on the Burnley to Todmorden road, as there's so much damn traffic, but before parting company we agreed to meet up for a pub lunch the following day, something I might not have suggested had the subject of Spain not reared its alluring head.

When I clumped into the kitchen in my cycling shoes Emma must have seen the reflection of a Spanish sunset or some such thing in my eyes, as she immediately asked me what I'd been up to.

"Nothing, well, cycling. I've arranged to meet Tim and Sue at the Shepherd's Rest tomorrow at one. Do you fancy it?"

"Yes, but I didn't think you were such great friends," she said, giving me one of her searching looks. I hadn't had an extra-marital affair by that time – or since, for that matter – but if I ever do it'll take Emma about a minute to find out about it.

"Well, seeing as they're living in Spain now, I thought it'd be nice to catch up."

"Right, OK."

"They won't be back till next summer, as they're on a bit of a tight budget, living just off his pension… and that," I said, conscious that this excess information would reveal what I'd been thinking about on the long, potholed descent into town.

"Are you plotting something?" she asked, her lovely brown eyes narrowing.

"Me?"

"I'm not talking to the fridge, Sam, and Luke's at his gran's."

"I'm not plotting nothing," I replied, as despite Emma's efforts to improve my mind, double negatives are rife in the building trade.. "Tim and me were just chatting about Spain and, well, I'd like to chat a bit more about it."

"That's nice. You never know, they might invite us out to stay."

"Yes, they might, though I think they've only got two bedrooms."

"Didn't they have a huge house up in Walsden?"

"Yes, but that's the secret, you see," I said, trying to keep the light of enthusiasm out of my eyes. "They've downsized and down-everythinged, so they can manage on his pension, for now."

"Sounds like a wise move," she said as she closed the dishwasher and turned to peruse me again. "Sam, you still look like you're going to break some astounding news. You haven't decided to start racing again, have you?"

"Course not."

"I mean, if you have, that's fine, but you know how time-consuming all the training is."

"It's nothing to do with cycling."

"Ha, but it *is* something!" she cried.

My Granddad had always warned me about marrying a woman cleverer than me, and this wasn't the first time that I'd saluted him up in heaven. Feeling tricked, I sat down and took my time taking my shoes off.

"Spit it out, Sam."

"Honestly, it's nothing... it's just... well, it does sound great living in Spain. I mean, look at the bloody weather here," I said, pointing out of the window into our small, moist garden.

"Sun's forecast tomorrow. We could go for a walk on the moors to work up an appetite for lunch."

Boring moors, I thought, and so far from the coast, or, more to the point, the Spanish coast, as Blackpool rarely tempted us to pack our buckets and spades and it was a long haul over to the more picturesque east coast.

"I suppose it might be nice to live abroad one day, but I fancy France," she said.

"Why France?" I asked, determined to work on that dreamy gleam in her eyes.

"Well, I speak the language for a start."

"Of course, but I bet there isn't much building work in France. There's *loads* in Spain right now."

"Good grief, what's Tim been saying to you?"

"Oh, just spelling out what a good time it is to move out there."

"For them, yes, and good luck to them."

This isn't a play, so I'll summarise the subsequent dialogue, which went on for a good half hour. According to Emma, I'd been smitten by a tempting but impractical idea, and though there was nothing wrong with that, it was important to separate dreams from reality, just like – and she actually cited this example – the drawing that Father Ted did for Father Dougal to help him to differentiate the two concepts. After laughing politely I then countered by saying that Tim had merely given me a bit of food for thought and that it wasn't written in stone that we were destined to spend our lives in that damp, sunless valley with bloody awful traffic on the main roads. Emma agreed that we weren't tethered at all, apart from the fact that our four parents – two each – lived in that damp and sunless valley and were all rather keen on spending a bit of time with their grandchild and, to a lesser extent, their children.

I parried this argument by saying that Luke was ours more than theirs and that, in any case, as we'd be rolling in money we'd be able to fly home two or three times a year to satisfy their grand-paternal urges, plus they could visit us in the spacious villa that our large income would provide us with.

"We can talk about this more later," Emma said with a note of finality.

"Yes."

"Like about fourteen years from now when Luke's done his A levels."

"Spoilsport."

"Maybe, but we're not talking about sport, though God knows you used to take that seriously enough. We're talking about our lives, which are going really well as far as I can see."

*(Please take note of that last sentence for future reference.)*

"True," I said, before giving her a kiss on the forehead behind which lay her huge but seemingly inflexible brain.

When we reached the country pub the next day my pro-Spain frenzy had calmed down a good deal. After all, I'd only visited the place twice and comfy tourist resorts hardly reflect the true nature of a country. I mean, I'd been to Egypt and Turkey too, but I didn't fancy living in either of those places, so when we sat down with Tim and Sue I was determined to take a back seat in our conversation and let the others lead it wherever they wished.

As we're nowhere near getting to Spain yet, let alone getting back, which is the whole point of this book, I'll speed things along somewhat, lest you begin to think that I'm going to spend about a hundred pages in Todmorden.

When someone has just emigrated, that topic naturally dominates proceedings, and as both Sue and Tim waxed lyrical about the Costa del Sol I was pleased to see Emma taking a lively interest in the accounts of their lives of active leisure. I was just thinking how that was all very well for them, when Tim said something very interesting and quite possibly decisive.

"Ay, it's a good life but, you know, I sometimes wish I had something more to do," he said, and Sue nodded in agreement, before pointing out that after working for thirty-odd years it seemed a bit strange to have no jobs to go to.

"To be honest, I think we'd enjoy it even more if we were working, maybe part time, as we're still relatively young," she said.

"Yes, if I had your building skills, Sam, I think I'd do a bit, but as I'm just a dumb copper, there's not much paid work I could do there."

"It'd be different for you two," Sue said. "You've both got skills that are really in demand out there."

At this point Emma looked at me a little suspiciously, as if I'd asked them to rehearse this little dialogue for our benefit, but as she has a built-in lie and bullshit detector, one glance at me told her that their comments were purely of their own volition. By the time we parted company and headed back into town, Emma was pretty pensive, so I made a point of talking about anything but Spain as we sat in the traffic waiting to reach the woefully inadequate miniature roundabout in the town centre.

"The traffic's getting worse here. It's taken us twenty minutes to drive about two miles," I said as she parked her car behind my van.

"I expect there's no traffic at all in Spain, is there?"

"Who said anything about Spain?"

"Ha, you didn't need to. OK, I'll have a think about everything they've told us, but I still think it's impractical."

"Yes, but there's nothing to stop us looking into it a bit."

So that's what we did, on the internet and in books. Back in 2005 there were far fewer books about people living in Spain and Chris Stewart's first one about his family's move to an old farmhouse in Andalusia is probably responsible for many an emigration. They didn't do it the easy way, as their house was practically a ruin and there was a stream between the house and the road, just to make things even more challenging. Neither he nor his wife had jobs and he had to depend on seasonal sheep-shearing work in Sweden in order to keep body and soul together.

You've probably read the book, and I'm sure there are hundreds of British people now living in Spain because of it, if not thousands. The moral of the story for us was that if they could overcome all those tremendous obstacles and make a go of it, it would be a piece of cake to go out there with a more feasible plan. Sometime in 2010 I turned that book around on the bookshelf, as every time I saw the spine it reminded me how much it had influenced us in our decision to up sticks and change our perfectly satisfactory lives. I still recommend it as an inspiring read, but just don't go putting your house on the market as soon as you've finished it, and ditto with the myriad of other books that are available nowadays, many no doubt written in the usually vain hope of making enough money to live as they'd dreamed they would when they first arrived in Spain.

Anyway, what with that book and all the articles we read online, the seeds that Tim and Sue had planted began to sprout within our heads and suddenly our lives didn't seem so hunky dory after all. When it rained we noticed it more. When winter arrived I cursed the cold and damp as I built a wall or clambered onto a roof, while Emma lamented the behaviour of a few of the kids at her school, having read that Spanish schools were wonderful places where lack of discipline and bullying didn't exist.

When the spring of 2006 was struggling to arrive I got into the silly habit of comparing the weather in Yorkshire to that in Malaga. 'Tomorrow it'll be eight degrees with showers here, while in Malaga it'll be eighteen with wall-to-wall sunshine,' I'd say to myself, making me dread the prospect of a perfectly normal working day that I'd have previously taken in my stride.

By the time Emma's school broke up for the summer we were both getting pretty hooked on the Spain idea, so we decided to go there on holiday. Following the advice we'd read, we hired a car for a fortnight at Malaga Airport and, after paying Tim and Sue a flying visit, we set off to explore. It was hot, almost too hot, but in an air conditioned car you don't notice it so much and as we headed north into the mountains we were delighted by the scenery, the white villages, and the relatively quiet roads.

We'd decided not to look for a home – a hypothetical home, as we were still far from making a decision on the matter – too near to Tim and Sue as we thought that we ought to strike out alone, and besides, neither of us really fancied living on the busy, multinational coast.

"A small town would be best," Emma said one day as we drove along the motorway north from Granada. "Big enough to have all the amenities, a choice of schools, and work for us both, but with nice countryside around it."

"Would you like to live here in Spain?" I asked Luke, who was five by that time.

"Why?" he asked, which I now think was a very pertinent question.

"Well, because it's nicer than Todmorden, isn't it?"

"Is it?"

"Of course it is. Look at the hills. Look at the sunshine."

"What about my friends at school?"

"Well, you'd be able to visit them," I said, having read all about how expat kids adapt instantly to everything you throw at them and always love Spain much more than Britain, though I'm not sure that the parents who wrote those articles had actually asked them, especially when there was an ulterior motive behind said article, like flogging houses or... well, mainly flogging houses.

As I write it seems to me that I might be beginning to overemphasise the potentially negative aspects of our gradual seduction, and thus using hindsight to distort what we actually felt at the time. We were, of course, delighted to be driving around Spain and the prospect of living there became more tempting the further we travelled. Emma had learnt some basic Spanish quite easily, as it's grammatically similar to French, and we were both struck by how friendly most people were, especially when addressed in their own tongue. It didn't occur to me then that if anyone asked me for directions back home I was always polite, cheerful and helpful, just like most other people in Todmorden and elsewhere. A smiling face in Spain seemed like a gift from the gods and a sure sign that life would be wonderful there, though I've no doubt that most people in Afghanistan, Hungary or Chile, for example, would be just as friendly and obliging.

One thing I didn't do on that trip was visit a building site. Had I done so, I might have realised how excruciating it is to work for hours under the burning sun, something I myself would have to do for up to four months a year. When you hop in and out of a hire car and sleep in air conditioned rooms you don't realise just how limiting the heat of the day can be.

Fancy a walk? Wait till the sun's going down or, better still, get up at the crack of dawn, but don't expect to enjoy a hike in the hills when the thermometer's pushing or exceeding thirty degrees. By contrast, some of the hotels we stayed at had pools, which was lovely after a hard day's driving and ambling around, sipping coffees or beers, eating tapas, and generally dossing about.

"This is the life," I said one evening as we strolled around the lovely town of Baeza in the province of Jaen.

"Hmm, I know this is a holiday, but can you imagine living somewhere like this and being able to stroll past these wonderful buildings every evening?" asked Emma.

"Yes, and it must be great for..." I was about to say cycling, but changed tack. "...walking around here."

"Yes, though there do seem to be rather a lot of olive trees."

"Yes, we'd live somewhere more wooded, I think."

So, we drove on from day to day, sizing up all the places we visited, which included Antequera, Valdepeñas, Cuenca, Albarracín, Segorbe, Játiva, Caravaca, Vélez-Rubio, Guadix and Alhama de Granada, the relentless sun illuminating each one of them and giving no hint as to how cold it can get in inland Spain, where most houses still lack central heating, at least in the southern half of the peninsula. We skirted the cities and admired the villages, and when we dropped off the car at the airport our stimulating tour had left us both completely sold on the idea of moving to Spain.

Luke said he'd enjoyed it, and he'd certainly been tickled by all the pampering he'd received, mostly in an amusingly unintelligible language.

"I want to go home now," he said at the airport.

"I don't," I said, more to Emma and myself. "I've got a tough job starting on Monday and the weather forecast's rubbish."

You can imagine that as I built an awkward garden wall on the edge of a ravine, with occasional cloudbursts to liven things up, each time I cast my mind back to our fortnight in Spain those halcyon days appeared in a very favourable light indeed.

"Good day, love?" Emma asked me one evening.

"Shit," I said, knowing that Luke wasn't around. "I'd rather be in Spain."

"Me too, but it'd be a big wrench, you know, especially for me."

"Why's that?"

"Well, I'd have to resign from work, of course, and I love my job."

"You can teach English there."

"Hmm, but it's not the same as teaching in a school."

"Well, when you learn the language you might be able to work in a school there."

"I looked into that. I'd have to do a degree in Spain, as it seems that they protect their jobs there. Oh, I wouldn't mind teaching English, don't get me wrong, and if I could get a job in a language school I guess I'd have groups of kids to teach, but the money's not very good."

"But we won't need as much there, and I should be able to make quite a bit, according to what I've read online. There's a real building boom now and it's showing no signs of slowing up. I doubt I'd be able to do the sort of work I like, not at first anyway, but I can lay bricks and tiles with the best of them," I said, making it clear that it wouldn't be ideal for me either.

"What about Luke? He's so settled at school now," she said, as although he didn't go to the school where she worked, we were both pleased that he was enjoying the one he was at.

"Oh, within a month he'd be so happy at his new school there that he'd have forgotten all about it."

"We'd have to move in the summer holidays then, as it'd make it easier for him, and for me too," she said a little ruefully.

"Yes, that would be the best time," I said, so from August 2006 onwards it seemed inevitable that we would move to Spain, and as autumn turned to winter we both became increasingly convinced that it would be our last one in England. That winter the cold was colder, the rain wetter and the ice more of a pain in the neck than ever before. Every time I de-iced the van I thought, I won't have to do this anymore. Every time I rubbed some life into my frozen fingers I thought, not much more of this for me now. During every shower I'd curse the heavens and remind myself that it never, ever rained in Spain, or not so you'd notice. When we occasionally went out for a meal in the evening we thought how nice it would be to be sitting outside on a terrace while Luke played with the other lovely, carefree children.

And all this because I'd gone for a short bike ride with Tim. If I hadn't picked up the phone that day, he'd have called another club mate and gone with him instead. Funnily enough, Tim and Sue had told us that they'd got the idea of going to Spain after visiting a retired colleague of hers in Denia, Alicante, and I guess it's often one fortuitous visit or encounter that makes most future expats begin to weigh up the pros and cons of Britain and Spain. In theory, Britain loses out every time, of course, and I sometimes think it's a wonder that Northern Europe hasn't been completely evacuated by now, in favour of Portugal, Spain, Italy and Greece.

It's only now that we've returned that I realise that many people actually like living in Britain and that when they express admiration or envy on hearing that someone is moving to sunnier climes, half the time they're just being polite, because when all's said and done, we are an extremely polite race. When you get the Spain bug though, like we did with a vengeance that winter, all things British turn as mushy as the melting snow and you can't imagine how you'd survived there for so long, let alone kidding yourself that you were actually happy.

# 2

Let's fast forward to July 2007 or I'll never get you out of the wonderful county of West Yorkshire which I so loathed by that time. The biggest decisions we'd had to make, of course, were whether to sell or rent out our house, and whether to buy or rent over in Spain. After careful consideration, we decided to rent first and buy later, once we were settled and established in the town of our choice.

Ha, you might think, so this dozy man and his slightly less dozy wife didn't suffer the trauma that other returning expats have had, as they hedged their bets by renting rather than buying. While this is true enough, I don't think it would have influenced any of our subsequent decisions, and would only have meant it taking longer for us to find our feet once we returned to Britain. It has even been said that some Britons are 'trapped' in Spain due to having property they can't sell, but this, if you'll pardon my language, is bollocks. If you're in war-torn Syria and can't get out, *then* you're trapped, but being from a country like ours means that even renegade expats are welcomed back with open arms and, at the time of writing, can soon find some sort of job.

Maybe that sounds like I'm making excuses for us not having gone the whole hog and selling up, but anyone thinking of going to live in Spain who has read this far, I strongly advise, even implore them *not* to sell up and *not* to buy a property until they've lived there for at least two years. This isn't an advice manual, but I can't resist sharing the odd pearl of my hard-earned wisdom from time to time. I mean, for goodness sake, we're talking about uprooting from the country where we've lived all our lives and starting afresh elsewhere, usually on the advice of a suntanned friend or two who happened to pop back for a fortnight.

Remember also that we all hate to admit our mistakes, so anyone who's plunged headlong into such a life-changing move is unlikely to confess that it's not what they expected. We certainly didn't, not for a long time anyway. I suppose it's a bit like spending thirty grand on a flashy car and then concealing the fact that the endless monthly payments don't justify the moderate amount of pleasure they get out of driving the thing to work and back. No, in my experience, life for British expats in Spain is great, great, great... until one day it turns into a nightmare and they have to come home right away.

How can this be? Did they not have an inkling during those three, seven or eleven years that life in Spain wasn't all it was cracked up to be? Of course they did, but they didn't admit it, *daren't* admit it, often not even to themselves. Then the proverbial shit hits the fan in one way or another and they come scurrying back home, feeling like complete failures and having to endure the pity and commiserations of their less adventurous loved ones.

I hope I'm not putting anyone off moving to Spain. Hey, if you're within spitting distance of retirement age, go for it, but even then I would rent and rent, rather than sell and buy, until you're sure that you like it more than your former home.

*Emma's just read this bit and told me to take it out and get back to the story, but what the heck, I'll leave it in as a foretaste of future outbursts of opinionated advice giving, which I'll try to keep to a minimum.*

By July 2007 we'd found a nice family to rent our house to through an agency, we'd sold the van and car and stored a lot of stuff in my parents' large house, and we'd rented a house just outside the town of Ontinyent, aka Onteniente, in Valencia. All this involved a good deal of work and planning, and we'd had to sell some of our furniture, rather cheaply, but we were all set and raring to go.

We'd settled on Ontinyent after extensive online research, carried out mostly by Emma, whose analytical powers are superior to my own. She tried to sort out the wheat from the chaff by reasoning that if someone was trying to sell something, their opinion was likely to be biased. She joined a couple of expat forums, perused a few more, and it turned out that as Ontinyent's once huge textile industry had suffered a slump since about the turn of the century, there were quite a few 'casitas', or second homes in the country, available for rent at reasonable prices, unlike the Malaga coast, for example, where Tim had told me that house prices had gone through the roof, dragging rental prices up with them.

On our road trip of the previous summer we'd driven quite close to Ontinyent and knew that the countryside was pleasant, with some great walking routes within a short drive. The town of thirty-odd thousand souls had quite a few expats by then, despite not being especially attractive or historic, and through an online forum Emma had contacted a British lady who'd agreed to help us with our paperwork and other linguistically challenging matters in return for small and moderate amounts of money. I'll call her Helen here, and will likewise modify the names of other people I'll be talking about, as it isn't my intention to intrude into mostly kind people's lives, or rub salt into the wounds of other returnees who will have suffered a harder homecoming than us.

Helen's assistance was absolutely invaluable and I would urge even those new expats who speak reasonable Spanish to enlist the help of a trustworthy veteran of wherever it is that you're going. Emma had approached Helen rather than the other way round, but if you do employ an established translator/interpreter, do make sure that their heart's in the right place, i.e, not solely in their purse or wallet, or, worse still, other people's purses or wallets. Helen sorted the house, found us a decent second-hand car to buy, got Luke into a nice school, and helped us with our residency and other paperwork with good-humoured efficiency. She was a godsend – I believe she still is – and enabled us to find our feet during that first summer.

We'd seen loads of photos and even a video of the house, so when we visited it for the first time we immediately knew it would do fine and signed the twelve month contract. Like many Spanish rental properties it was furnished, ours in a more modern way than most, as the owners had let it very reluctantly due to him losing his job at a textile factory. You might already be thinking that a town with substantial unemployment wasn't the best place for a builder to go, but Helen had assured us that urban building was still going on and that the increasing number of expats often wanted to reform the properties they'd snapped up from the recession-hit locals.

As for Emma's prospects, it appeared that the Spanish middle classes had an overwhelming desire to have their kids learn English, as even then there were too few graduate opportunities within the country to satisfy the growing number of engineers, doctors, architects and suchlike. In any case, we'd decided to allow ourselves the seven weeks until Luke started school to settle in and put out a few feelers regarding work, so we weren't too worried about how to earn our daily bread just yet.

The house was about a mile to the north of the town, where the land had been divided up into irregular plots during the town's boom years of the 1960s and 1970s. There were a few impressive houses, but most were like ours; modest white bungalows with red-tiled roofs and less land than the planning laws had required, but it transpired that folk hadn't worried too much about such minor matters back then, and as the local politicians had also built illegally, the bulldozers were unlikely to move in, though things had become much stricter by the time we arrived. I would think carefully about buying one of those houses though, as you never know what obstacles might appear if you decided to sell it, though it would probably go through smoothly enough.

Though most houses had swimming pools ours didn't, which probably saved us at least a hundred quid a month in rent, if not more. I soon rigged up an outdoor shower, which refreshed us well enough during that first summer, and we were both pleased about our frugal economic policy, even before we started looking for work. Our house had three bedrooms, one bathroom, a large lounge cum dining room, a small study, a modern kitchen, and a large covered porch facing south. It had about half a football pitch worth of land, with a few plum and cherry trees, some hardy bushes, and quite a bit of gravel. We had a good view of the town and the scenic mountain range to the south, while behind us to the north, just past the remaining houses, another, less wooded range stretched away from east to west.

Being out in the country, or suburbs, we didn't meet too many people at first, though we did get to know the neighbours on one side of us, whose two kids – a boy and girl of seven and nine – soon took Luke in hand and invited him to play in their pool. Though Juan and Carmen, their parents, were friendly and communicative, the fact that they preferred to communicate in English put a bit of a damper on our Spanish learning initiative, as no matter how often Emma began a conversation in Spanish, Carmen would continue it in English, while Juan mostly nodded approvingly. My own Spanish was still very rudimentary, despite Emma's efforts to share her ever-increasing knowledge with me, so we didn't spend nearly as much time with them as we would have if they'd spoken to us in their own language, or one of their languages, as many people in the area speak Valenciano, though we did find that on spotting a foreigner they soon switched to Castellano, or Spanish.

"What shall we do today?" Emma asked me one morning on the porch a few days after settling in. By that time we'd bought everything we needed for the house, filled our cupboards, fridge and freezer, and were raring to go.

"Good question. Everything's more or less shipshape here now, though I'd quite like to extend that patio over to the lemon tree."

"But it's not our house, Sam."

"True, but it wouldn't cost that much."

"Hmm, hang fire a bit till we see if we like it here."

"We're bound to like it. I mean, we're in the country, handy for town, and the house is as sound as a pound. What is there not to like? A location like this back in England would cost a packet. Let's just sit here and enjoy it."

"I'll get the Spanish books and we'll study till Luke gets back from next door."

"OK."

"And get out of the sun. You look like a tomato."

"I'll be as brown as a berry soon."

"Since when were berries brown? You'll go from tomato to beetroot and damage your skin in the process," she said, never having been much a sun worshiper, and nor had I, for that matter, but when in Rome…

"How are we going to meet people living up here?" she asked me a while later, after stretching my grey matter with a few verb conjugations.

"We've already met Juan and Carmen."

"Yes, and they're fine, but they'll hardly be a stepping stone into society if they speak to us in English all the time, and a lot of the other houses seem to be empty."

"I guess when we start working we'll meet more folk."

"If we don't meet more folk we won't *get* any work. Maybe summer wasn't the best time to come out, after all, as the town's pretty dead."

"Let's just chill out like I bet Tim and Sue did," I said, easing back my reclining chair.

"Hmm, I'll try, but I feel like we should be getting into the thick of it rather than sitting on our arses."

That snippet of conversation makes it sound like we were lamenting our fate right from the start, and that wasn't the case, but in a book of this nature I'm evidently going to highlight the potential shortcomings of our decision. That evening, for instance, we drove into town and strolled around the park, before drinking a couple of beers at the café there while Luke played with the other kids, who seemed fascinated by the gibberish he talked, though one girl of about seven soon cottoned on and spoke a few words of English to him. What we'd read seemed to have been spot on regarding children's adaptability, but what about us grown-ups?

"That family over there look English," Emma said when we'd been there for about an hour. "We should go and have a chat with them."

"They might think we're imposing," the reserved Englishman in me said.

"Maybe, and I really want to get to know Spanish people first. I don't want us to be the type of expats who don't learn the language properly. Just imagine if a year from now when Luke speaks it like a native, we're still trying to string sentences together. What a fool I'd feel when I saw the other parents, like when kids came round for a birthday party or something."

"You Spanish is pretty good already. I'm the one who's lagging behind, but I can't absorb it from books like you can."

"Hmm, I know quite a bit, but I can't tell what the hell they're saying at that table over there. We're going to have to watch a lot of Spanish TV to get more listening practice."

"So are we not going to get English telly?" I asked hopefully.

"Definitely not. We've got plenty of DVDs in English and what's the point in coming here if we're not going to try to integrate?"

"I'll need to meet Brits to find work," I said, hoping she wasn't going to go completely native on me.

"Of course, and I want to meet a few too, but I don't want to get into some bloody expat set."

As you can see, Emma takes thing pretty seriously, even friendship choices, though two years previously the idea of going to live in Spain wouldn't have crossed her mind in a month of Sundays. As for me, I was keen to meet people to go out cycling with and I didn't really care if they were Spanish, British or from the Solomon Islands, though I supposed a Spanish cycling pal would be best. On the second Sunday after our arrival, I ventured out on my bike just after sunrise, and though I enjoyed the gruelling forty mile circuit through Moixent and past Fontanars dels Alforins, I didn't meet a soul and arrived home gasping for breath and water, having finished my large bottle about an hour from home.

"Bloody hell, it's hot," I said as I collapsed onto a chair."

"You should go out earlier."

"I'd have to get lights for the bike. Still, it's a bit too hot now, but it's going to be great during the rest of the year."

"Yes, you know, I think the Spanish summer's going to be a bit like the English winter in some ways," Emma said.

"What? Have you been drinking this early in the day?"

"Ha, listen. Back home in winter there are things you can't do, or don't want to do, because of the weather. I think the summer's a bit like that here. In the heat of the day we're sort of confined to barracks, but, like you say, the rest of the year's going to be great, so it'll more than make up for it."

"Yes, a month from now it'll start cooling down and I guess we'll go home for two or three weeks next summer, so that'll break it up," I said, immediately thinking about the slightly vexed grandparents who Luke had left behind, and who we'd asked not to visit for at least three months until we'd found our feet. My parents, who lived in Todmorden, were the least pleased about us going, maybe because they'd got used to seeing Luke, and us, several times a week. Emma's parents still lived near Halifax, so our departure was a little easier to bear, and they were that much nearer to Leeds-Bradford airport too. In both cases it really was going to be Luke who they missed though, almost as if they'd lavished all the love they could on us and now relished a new outlet for it.

Still, we intended to go home at least twice a year and expected them to visit a couple of times too, so they'd be getting some quality time with him, and us, about every three months. At the time it did make me wonder about those people who emigrate to Australia, New Zealand and other such far-flung places. That really must be a wrench, unless they don't particularly want to see their families, in which case it's a pretty shrewd plan. Emma and I did get on with our folks though, so even Spain seemed quite distant at times, especially that first summer, as there's only so much sunbathing you can do and it threatened to become something of a waiting game as the scorching days passed slowly by.

We went down to the park in town – known as La Glorieta – about three evenings a week, and through a cunning plan of Emma's we managed to meet some people. As Luke always took off as soon as we arrived at the café tables, not being nearly as shy as us when it came to socialising, Emma decided to use his instant friendships as a means of introduction.

"Look, he's playing with those Spanish kids on the swings. If they go near their table I'll nip over with his top and say something to the parents," Emma said one evening when a cooler breeze began to waft through the trees.

"It's a brave move, but go for it," I said with a hint of irony.

"Or better still, you go."

"I probably won't understand what they say to me."

"Chicken," she said, before seizing her opportunity.

There were two couples at the table and I soon saw Emma chatting away to them. I really hoped none of them would start speaking English, but I think her Spanish was good enough by then to make doing so rather rude. After a while she beckoned to me, and as I saw one of the blokes pulling two chairs up, I picked up our drinks and strolled over, feeling nervous about our forthcoming chat. I knew enough to introduce myself and say a few pleasantries, but it was Emma who answered their questions and I understood her Spanish as I was used to hearing it at home.

She told them where we lived and what we planned to do, whereupon one of the men, a slim, tanned chap of about my age called Antonio, pulled a face and said that things weren't too hot in the building trade, or words to that effect. Emma then said that I hoped to find work among the foreign community too, and he replied that I might have more luck there. Him, his wife Cristina and all three kids left shortly afterwards, leaving Luke without playmates and us with Álvaro and Chelo for company.

It turned out that Álvaro was a local policeman, while Chelo, his girlfriend, lived in Alcoy, a larger town some twenty miles south of Ontinyent. Álvaro looked about forty-five – fifty, it turned out – while Chelo was a pretty, curvy lady at least ten years younger than him. Álvaro did most of the talking and we immediately knew, or hoped, that he was the sort of pleasant, communicative local who we so needed to befriend. Rather than picking our brains about why we'd come to live there and suchlike, he and Emma talked in a general way, as did Chelo to a lesser extent, while I interjected words and grunts of agreement from time to time when I understood what they were talking about.

He approved of our, or rather Helen's, choice of school for Luke, before telling us that his own two daughters were grown up and both had good jobs in the town. He was more upbeat than his friend Antonio about the building trade, as although Ontinyent wasn't growing as fast as other towns, due to its practically moribund textile industry, there was still plenty of building going on there and in the surrounding villages. As prices were rising ceaselessly, he said, many of his friends and colleagues were investing in properties on the coast, in Benidorm and other places, and although he'd thought about it, he had a hunch that the boom wouldn't last forever and that it was too late to buy now. Wise words indeed in view of what was to happen the following year.

As Luke was getting tired, still unused to his much changed sleeping hours, we decided to make a move, but not before Álvaro had drawn a map showing us how to get to his casita on the opposite side of town from ours, and asked us to give him a call and pay him a visit sometime soon. On the short drive home Emma filled me in on the bits of conversation I'd missed and we both agreed that it had been a stroke of luck to bump into such a friendly, helpful chap.

"He's a lone wolf," said Emma as the tyres of our Seat Ibiza crackled onto the gravel.

"What makes you say that?" I asked, as the slim man of about five eight, with short hair, normal teeth and a kindly face didn't look at all like a wolf.

"I mean it in a nice way, but this is my guess. He had a difficult marriage and divorce and now likes to keep his independence."

"What about Chelo?"

"As they said, they don't live together."

"I missed that bit."

"Well, I think that after having been under the thumb for so many years, he's sort of come out of his shell and likes to meet all sorts of people. That's why he took up ballroom dancing, where he met Chelo."

"I missed that bit too."

"Hmm, they spoke Valenciano to each other and Castellano to us."

"Did they?"

"Yes, it's pretty similar and I can understand some of it, but I guess it's hard for them to speak to each other in Spanish. We must go and see him though. Not just because he's nice, but being a local cop he'll know everything that's going on around here."

Three evenings later we were sitting outside Álvaro's small, old-fashioned casita drinking the sangría that he'd made. It transpired that Emma had been just about spot on in her assessment of his life experience. He'd had a very protracted and painful separation and divorce and had no intention of getting hitched again.

"You women are nice to be with," he said to Emma, in Spanish, of course. "But a man needs to keep his independence. Chelo would like me to move into her big flat in Alcoy, but I prefer to live mostly in this little place that my father built," he said, quite slowly and with helpful gestures.

"But you do much work here?" I asked in my Indian Spanish.

"Yes, I built a second storey and also a new bathroom. My parents never lived here, but it is big enough for me, and I entertain myself on the land," he said, pointing to the elongated allotment where all kinds of vegetables were planted, as well as several kinds of fruit trees. "Next I will build a workshop over there to store my implements."

"I'll help you," I said.

"Ha, thank you, but I cannot afford to pay a professional builder," he said, rubbing his finger and thumb together, shaking his head, and smiling.

"No, not for money," I replied, rubbing *my* finger and thumb together and shaking my head. "My hands now are…"

"…getting soft," Emma added helpfully.

"I need do work. I help you. It fun for me," I said, more or less, earning myself a slap on the back and another glass of the rather strong brew.

"Remember you are driving," Emma said in Spanish. "And Álvaro is a policeman."

"Ha, don't worry. There are no checks tonight and two or three glasses will do no harm," he said, which I don't suppose a copper would say back home.

After a light supper and more chatter, we collected Luke from the cabbages and headed home, but the next day I would be back, bright and early, wearing work clothes and raring to go. I knew it wouldn't be easy for the two of us to communicate, but Emma had encouraged me to go alone in order to practise my Spanish and 'bond' with Álvaro, who, she said, although a great admirer of womankind, was essentially a man's man.

"Go on your bike and me and Luke will come along later," she said that night in bed. "It's good of you to help him and I'm sure he's worth getting to know better."

"I didn't suggest helping him with any ulterior motives in mind," I said. "I really do feel like getting stuck into something."

"I know, and it's a shame there's nothing for you to do here. You know, I think Álvaro's a bit of a one-off. I get the feeling that the locals in general are a bit standoffish."

"Really?"

"Yes, I might be wrong, but when we go shopping or out somewhere I can't help feeling that they could be a bit friendlier and more... well, forthcoming. I'm sure if a Spanish couple moved to Todmorden some folk would be a bit more curious about them."

"That can't be true, not according to what we've read, anyway. In theory the Spanish are jolly, friendly and welcoming, while we English are dull, cold and remote," I said with a chuckle.

"*We* aren't."

"No, I guess not."

So, at about eight the next morning I cycled up the steep, narrow lane to Álvaro's casita and found him helping the driver of a builder's truck to back into his driveway, which he did with about an inch to spare on either side. The truck contained breeze blocks and I was all for cutting the plastic off the pallets and getting cracking.

"No, we'll have coffee first, Sam," Álvaro said once the truck had left the pallets and gone, before propelling me onto the small terrace with his hand on the small of my back. It felt strange to be manhandled in such a way, and though I'm sure it's true that Spaniards are more tactile than us – they could hardly be less so – Álvaro was especially fond of patting and prodding me around, maybe to supplement the verbal communication that we both found difficult. Not being a teacher, it took him a while to gauge just how much Spanish I knew, but he soon realised that I probably had a vocabulary of about two hundred words and adjusted his speech accordingly. When I spoke he usually understood me right away and never tried to correct me, which was just as well at that stage, as my mind was working hard enough just to understand him and formulate some sort of reply.

As he'd already laid the foundations for his workshop, using, he said and mimed, bits of an old bicycle and other metal debris to strengthen the concrete, he was soon shovelling sand and cement into his little mixer and it wasn't long before I'd laid the first layer of blocks.

"You are very fast and very good," he said to me as I wiped the sweat from my brow, though his skin was still bone dry, despite his energetic mixing and carrying.

"I like it," I replied, and it did feel great to make myself useful doing what I knew best, though I'd have preferred to use bricks or, better still, blocks of stone.

I won't try to transcribe the bulk of our conversation over the next few hours, as it would make very tedious reading indeed, but we chatted and gestured as we worked and by the time Emma and Luke arrived in the car I'd learnt a lot about Ontinyent and our prospects there.

Álvaro said that the people of the town were indeed rather insular and that there was a saying in surrounding villages such as Agullent, Albaida and Bocairent regarding the townsfolk. 'Ontinyent, mala gent,' they said, which though more rhythmic than the English version – 'Ontinyent, bad people' – was a pretty damning verdict. Álvaro later told us that he had arrived in the town at the age of fifteen from the village of Chella, twenty-odd miles to the north, his parents having been lured there by the plentiful work in the factories. They had never integrated much, he said, partly because they weren't Valenciano speakers, so he'd made a special effort to learn it properly as soon as he could. He'd become a local policeman at the ripe old age of seventeen, at a time when most men scorned the job as they could earn much more in the textile factories.

"Now many people are jealous of me, because I have a safe job and they have no job at all," he said after changing into his uniform and strapping on his pistol holster, prior to starting work at 2pm.

"Have you ever used that?" Emma asked him as Luke looked on in wonder at his transformation from a scruffy builder into some sort of soldier.

"Once I felt threatened and drew it, but no, I've never had the opportunity to use it," he said with an enigmatic smile.

"Police not have pistol in England," I said.

"I know. I like it. It makes me feel safe."

"I bet it does," said Emma.

"Now there are some immigrants from South America and Eastern Europe living in town, and though most of them are peaceful and hard-working there is a troublesome element too, especially when they get drunk. Now I must go. Tomorrow I don't work, so I will make a paella for us."

"Fantástico," I said, as I'd already agreed to put in another mini-shift.


"Did you manage to understand each other OK?" Emma asked me as she drove carefully down the hill, as I'd popped my dismantled bike in the back.

"Yes, and he'll spread the word that there's a great new builder in town, which is brilliant. He thinks you should check out the language schools and maybe put up adverts for private classes in the supermarkets and other shops, but we can't expect any work till September, as August is very much a holiday month."

"Well done," she said, patting my leg. "Álvaro could be our passport into society, you know."

"Yes, it's a good thing we met him."

# 3

How true that was we were to discover over the coming weeks. After helping him to finish the walls of his workshop over the following three days – he still hadn't decided what kind of roof he was going to put on it – I cycled up to see him at least twice a week, he occasionally called on us, and we sometimes met up with him and Chelo in the café in the park. The local police are like traditional bobbies who walk the beat and he soon checked out the building scene for me. He found out that the two biggest companies, Construcciones Francés and Mancebo González, weren't hiring, but he promised to speak to the smaller builders too when he came across them.

For the rest of the summer he was the hub of our social life and although he introduced us to more local people, none seemed anxious to draw us into their circles, though Álvaro did reiterate that the Valencianos weren't like the Andaluces, who were reputed to be more sociable and hospitable.

"Here for many years the people thought only about making money. Money to build their casitas, and to take part in the fiestas in great style. Now many cannot earn money, or very much, but they don't know how to adapt to their new circumstances," he said one evening at our house.

"I see. The fiestas start soon, don't they?" Emma said, as we'd seen and heard a lot about these Fiestas de Moros y Cristianos.

"Sí," he said with a big sigh. "You will see little of me this week as I have to work more hours."

"What parts of the fiesta are worth seeing?" she asked.

"The Alardos procession on Thursday evening is amusing, and the main procession on Friday is impressive, though very long. You must walk down as it will be impossible to park," he said without much enthusiasm.

"Do you not like them because you have to work?" Emma asked.

"Not only that. A few colleagues do take time off for them, and I could have joined one of the festero groups, known as comparsas, many years ago, but it is not for me."

"What don't you like about it?"

"Oh, the processions I mentioned are fine, but the festeros lunch and dine together every day for over a week. Ugh, forty men sat around tables, eating, drinking and talking rubbish. I am too much of an individualist to enjoy such celebrations. Also it is very expensive. A festero can easily spend a thousand euros each year, and much more if they wish to have a special role. To be the captain of one's comparsa can cost as much as a new car. Such a waste of money and merely an excuse to show off and get drunk all week." He shook his head sadly. "*But*, Luke will like it a lot. For children it is thrilling the first time."

"Only for children?" I asked.

"You will see. Wave to me if you see me sweating in my uniform."

The processions did prove to be impressive, especially the grand 'Entrada' of first the Christian and then the Moorish armies. We watched it for a while from the end of the old main street, where people sat patiently on wooden chairs and benches for hours on end as the different comparsas marched past, each followed by a brass band. After a while we moved up the much wider Daniel Gil Avenue to get a better view, occasionally nipping into a bar to buy drinks.

"It's lasting a long time," I said as the fourth Moorish comparsa filed along, all looking ever so serious as they marched slowly past, swaying to the vaguely eastern music, some smoking huge cigars, which I thought a dubious historical detail.

"Yes, I think the Christians took about four hours, so this lot will be just as long," Emma said, getting a bit tired of being joggled by the crowds. "I guess they've all paid, so they all want to take part. It's great, but I get the feeling that they do it more for their own enjoyment than to please the crowd. Look at him there." She pointed to a fat, sweaty chap who, like many others, had grown a beard for the occasion, unlike the Christians, who presumably never wore them back in the day. "God, he looks so solemn and self-important. They really do take it seriously."

"I think that bloke on the next row's pissed," I murmured in her ear, after observing his spaced out eyes and leering mouth. "It looks like the two on either side are holding him up. He might get sacked and spend the rest of his life in disgrace. I bet he'll commit hara-kiri with that big sword of his."

"What's hara-kiri?" asked Luke.

"Er, a sort of drink."

"It seems a bit masonic to me. You might have to join a comparsa if you want to get building work," Emma said with a slightly supercilious chuckle.

"No thanks. I'm an individualist like Álvaro. Oh, he told me that one year he was called out because a woman poured a bottle of bleach onto a tableful of them from her fourth floor flat. It seems that the constant noise for days on end had driven her nuts."

"Did you understand all that?"

"Yes, but it took him a while to explain it, and he's a good actor. More and more people go away for the week these days, he said, as it's just too much."

"It's been too much for Luke," she said as he swayed against her leg. She picked him up and started to make her way down the avenue.

"I think I'm going to have to tout for work among the expat community," I said as I carried Luke up the steep hill to our house.

"Yes, it looks like there's nothing doing among the local builders. I think they're a bit wary about employing foreigners here. I mean, there are supposed to be quite a lot of them around, including Brits, but you never see any working in the shops or anywhere, apart from maybe the odd South American girl in the bars."

"I believe the economic immigrants work mostly in the country, as the locals don't want to do that sort of work, and I guess the others don't need to work."

"We do," she said, before taking Luke off my hands for a while.

"Yes, we do. It's been great meeting Álvaro, but we need to get to know some other expats too, and quick. It'll be September next week and we need to start earning some money."

"There's that place on the old main street which is run by Brits. We ought to go there," she said, referring to a small bar on the busy, narrow shopping street leading to the town hall.

"Yes, but let's wait till the fiestas are over. Then we'll see who the regulars are."

"More fiestas tomorrow," said Luke sleepily.

"We'll see. You'll be starting school in two weeks. Are you looking forward to that?" his mum asked him.

"Yes, I want to see more children."

"Good," I said, relieved that he hadn't demanded to be taken back to Todmorden and the security that we'd so recklessly left behind.

On the following Wednesday morning I strode boldly into the abovementioned bar, intent on making friends and influencing people. Emma had decided that I ought to go alone and said that she'd pop in another time, as that way we'd be more likely to get chatting to people.

"As far as I know it's the only British bar in town, so we have to make the most of it," she'd said the previous evening after evidently having given much thought to the matter. "We've got five combinations we can use."

"What?"

"You, me, me and Luke, you and Luke, and all three of us."

"What are you on about, love?" I asked, perplexed.

"It's simple sociology, Sam. In different situations you meet different people. We need to become regulars whether we like it or not, and if all three of us go we'll make a self-sufficient family unit who folk might not be so keen to intrude on. If you go and lean on the bar and guzzle a few beers you'll meet one type of person. If I go and have a couple of coffees I'll meet another type. Do you see what I mean?"

"Why don't you go and guzzle beer and I'll go and sip coffee?"

"Because you're looking for building work and I'm looking for classes. It's horses for courses. Builders are boozers and teachers are prim and proper like me," she said with a grin. "Though I guess an expat bar isn't the best place to find English students," she added thoughtfully. "Still it's all about making contacts."

"Aren't you being a bit cynical about all this? Shouldn't we just go and be ourselves."

"When we were being ourselves back in Tod, how often did we go out?"

"Er, once a week, if that."

"Exactly. We're a home-loving couple, me and you, but that won't do now."

"OK, but you've forgotten one combination."

"Which?"

"Luke on his own."

"We'll send him along to beg if we don't find any work."

Many a true word is often spoken in jest. I don't mean about sending Luke out to beg, but about the rather insular way in which we were used to living. We had friends of course, one or two of whom might get a mention in the course of my story, but we liked our own company so much that we'd got used to staying at home, and when we did go out it was usually for a walk, maybe followed by a pub meal somewhere, often just the three of us. We saw our families quite a lot, as I've said, so we just didn't have the time, inclination or energy left to do much socialising. We knew we'd have to change our lifestyle quite a bit, especially at first, so Emma's pedantic strategy wasn't as daft as it sounds, not for us.

So, I strolled into the bar with a big smile on my face and I suppose I should paint a picture of the place and the people in it, but I won't because it just seems too intrusive. I know Álvaro won't mind my portrayal of him, as nine years on we're still good friends and he says to go ahead and describe him, warts and all, but when it comes to describing other people we met, and not always in a flattering way, it's just too rude to be overly specific. In writing this book I'm not looking for controversy, so no-one will find much material for gossip here, I'm afraid.

I bid the owner good morning, ordered a glass of beer, and picked up the copy of the Costa Blanca News that lay on the bar. There were a couple of couples drinking coffee and a big, crimson-faced bloke sitting further down the bar, so after downing half my beer I decided to have a chat with him.

"Hi, mate. Have you lived here long?" was my opening gambit.

"A while," he said in a southern accent, probably London or thereabouts.

"We only moved here in July."

"Right."

"We've rented a house up past the religious school."

"Ah," he said with a nod, before turning away to sip his coffee.

"We're both looking for work now. I'm a builder."

"Afraid I must be off," he said after finishing his drink, leaving a coin on the bar, and slipping from his stool in one seamless movement.

"Bye," I said to his back as he stepped out onto the street, before checking that no-one was looking and sticking out my tongue.

So, that first rather brief conversation wasn't a great confidence booster, but I finished my beer and ordered a second. After making it last for as long as I could, nobody else had entered who looked the least bit inclined to talk, so I paid up and took my leave. Maybe I'd been wrong to assume that every fellow expat would take a modicum of interest in a new arrival, but it was still disappointing and not at all like the expat bars I'd read about, where pleasant banter and constant exchanging of information were the order of the day, as if Brits abroad were one big team, a bit like Team GB with cotton shorts instead of lycra ones.

Rather than being too thorough and chronological, which might result in one of those eight volumes of autobiography that I mentioned, I'll tell you about my next encounter in the British bar, as I'll call it, which took place two days later. I went along in the afternoon in a less than positive mood, as Emma had visited both language schools that morning and been told that they didn't need more teachers, though one of them did take her CV and told her that they'd call her if any teaching hours became available.

I sat at the bar, ordered a coffee, and became so plunged in thought that when a thin, tallish man in his sixties addressed me, he startled me a little.

"Are you living around here?" he asked in a north-eastern accent that I couldn't quite place.

"Er, yes, me and the wife have rented a casita up past the Concepción school."

"We've been here for five years now," he said, his beady brown eyes indicating that I ought to question him further. His skin was like old leather, so he'd obviously put in a lot of time out in the sun.

"Oh, whereabouts do you live?"

"We bought a casita up beyond San Rafael," he said, referring to a working class district to the north of the river, which meant that his house would be to the west of ours, on the other side of a deep, dry gully.

"And how are you liking it?"

"All right, apart from the fact that the escritura for the house is a mess," he said, referring to the deeds.

"Oh, why's that?"

"Well, there was no problem buying it, though they wanted a quarter of the money in cash, but we've found out that there are some irregularities and that if anyone needed a mortgage to buy it, they'd struggle to get one."

"Right, so are you trying to sell it?"

"No, but that's not the point, is it?"

"Isn't it?"

He shook his balding head and clamped his lips together, before looking at me as if I were a small child. "No, because it means that we're stuck there."

"Do you like it?"

"Oh, it's fine. Good views, a great pool and garden, but what if we wanted to move? I can't sleep at night for thinking about it, and what makes it worse is that its value is going up all the time. It's like sitting on a goldmine that you can't exploit."

"Hmm, but I guess all houses are going up in price."

"Not as much as ours. Prime location, you see, and what if we wanted to move back to England?"

"Do you?"

"Course not, we wouldn't go back to that miserable dump in a million years, but what if we wanted to, or needed to?"

"Er, well, I guess you'd have to sell it to someone who wouldn't need a mortgage," I said, beginning to feel like a counsellor or financial adviser, rather than an out of work builder.

"Not everyone's got two hundred and seventy grand lying around," he said with a slightly gloating smile. "It only cost us a hundred and forty, though we had the pool built later."

"That's good," I replied, hoping it was the right thing to say.

"Heated."

"Sorry?"

"The pool, it's heated."

"Great."

"That buys us another couple of months swimming."

"So can you swim all year round?"

On hearing this, his eyes widened for the first time, before he shook his head again, sadly this time. "You can tell you're new. It gets bloody nippy here in winter. We're quite high up, you see, so it's not like down on the coast. They don't tell you that when you come out in summer to look around."

"No, I don't suppose they do," I said, though as Emma had printed out the annual mean temperatures, we'd known more or less what to expect.

"So we installed central heating. We're as snug as bugs now."

"Great."

"Though it costs a fortune to run, as the house isn't as well insulated as it ought to be."

"No? I'm a builder and I could come and–"

"But we manage, as we've got four pensions coming in," he said, before ordering himself another café con leche.

"What do you do?" I asked rather pointedly, as the smug twit was starting to get on my nerves a bit.

"What do you mean?"

"Well, what do you do each day? We're new, you see, so we still don't know how people spend their time."

"We don't *do* anything. We're retired."

"Don't you get bored?"

"Of course not. We swim, sunbathe, go out for meals, do a spot of gardening, watch a little TV."

"English TV?"

"Of course, you don't expect us to watch the gibberish on the Spanish channels, do you?"

"No," I said, thinking how wonderful and informative a typical evening of viewing could be back home, though Emma and I had tried not to overdo it. "How are you getting on with the language?"

"Oh, we get by."

"I'm struggling with the verbs right now," I said, praying he'd say what I wanted him to say, so at least I'd have something funny to tell Emma to cheer her up. I expected him to say that you didn't need verbs, but he said something even better.

"You only need eight."

"Sorry?"

"Eight verbs. Ir, comer, beber, pagar, comprar, vender, querer and gustar," he said, pronouncing each one in perfect English.

"Hmm, yes, I guess they're the most important ones, but there are a hell of a lot of conjugations, aren't there?"

"No need to worry about them. If you use them with I, you, we, or whatnot, and yesterday, today, tomorrow, next week, and so on, you can make yourself perfectly understood, as long as you've got plenty of vocabulary too. Jane and I had it sussed after the first year and we've never looked back."

Or forward, I thought. "That's good to know. I think I've been making it more difficult than I needed to. Oh, if you ever need any building work doing, please let me know. I'm Sam, by the way."

"Brian." He shook my big, meaty hand very hard with his thin, bony one. "Everything's shipshape at our place, apart from the damn deeds."

"OK, I just thought I'd mention it."

"Give me a card anyway. I might come across someone who needs something doing, and you can trust the local builders about as far as you can throw them."

"Er, I left my cards at home, but I'll pop down with one for you soon. Have you had problems with the local builders?"

"Not exactly problems, in fact they've been quite good, but I've always suspected they charged me more than they would a native."

"I see," I said, before taking out my cardless wallet.

I know, I know, both Emma and I should have had cards made weeks ago, but with the town being so dead I guess we'd been lulled into lethargy, planning to spring into life on the first of September. That date had passed and we still hadn't got our act together, so after paying for our coffees, to Brian's surprise and gratification, I said goodbye and walked quickly home.

"Anything doing down there?" Emma asked me when I trotted up the steps to the porch. "Have you robbed a bank?" she added on seeing how sweaty I was.

"No, funny meeting in the bar... tell you later... we need to get some cards made," I said, still panting.

"I know, I've been drafting them just now." She patted the laptop on the table beside her. "Do you want to put the same on yours as on the cards you used back home?"

"More or less, but I'm not sure how to get hold of scaffolding here yet, so we'd better keep it general. You know, all kinds of building work carried out, and maybe a few more details."

"Then there's the small matter of getting yourself a van."

"Yes, Álvaro knows the best place to buy a good second-hand van," I said, before going inside to grab a towel.

The reason I'd put off buying a van wasn't due to laziness, but because I'd thought I might get a job working for someone else, in which case I'd planned to buy a moped. As Álvaro's continuing enquiries hadn't come up with anything yet, I'd have to go down the self-employment route, though Helen, who we were still emailing regularly, had said that the monthly payments were quite high and that I ought to get at least one big job before I went legal, whereupon she would help me to sort everything out. I had all my tools, by the way, as we'd had six square metres of stuff delivered in a removal van, including a couple of chairs that we liked, two computers, a music system, my bike and Luke's, clothes, shoes, bedding, some books, CDs and DVDs, Luke's toys, and other bits and bats.

By the time I'd had a refreshing outdoor shower, Emma had printed out drafts of our respective business cards. Hers were in Spanish, offering English and French classes, while mine were in

English and Spanish, offering general building services, no job too big or too small etc.

"Now for some flyers," she said, her fingers already flying around the keyboard.

"Flyers, yes, that's a good idea. Where will we put them?"

"In all the shops and bars that'll stick them up, on lampposts, anywhere visible. I'll make them a quarter page with bold text, nice and simple. Pretty much like the cards really. Oh, shit."

"What?"

"We've only got one mobile," she said, slapping the glass-topped table in disgust. That won't do. If you nip round and pick Luke up from the neighbours', we'll pop into town and get one for you, then put the number on your cards and flyers and take them for printing tomorrow morning."

"OK, back soon."


"We could call in at our favourite bar now," I said after we'd bought a cheap mobile phone in a shop half way up Daniel Gil Avenue.

She grimaced. "We could, but let's go to the park instead."

Emma had also visited the British bar twice by then and hadn't been impressed. She said she felt like she'd stepped into a Benidorm bar – a place where she'd never been, by the way – and that after a brief exchange with the friendly owner, she'd found her coffee glass empty and hadn't the heart to order another one.

"The trouble with you is that you're a bit of a snob," I said half an hour later in the park, after telling her about my chat with Brian, which she'd found both funny and sad, but mainly funny.

"No, I'm not."

"Yes, you are. Being a teacher you're more used to cultivated company and you can't tune into the common man any more," I said, determined to tease her out of her grumpy mood.

"Ha, if you'd heard some of the conversations in the staffroom back in Tod you wouldn't say that. Besides, it's just not true. We both come from working class families and I think we know how to talk to folk from all walks of life. I think what bothers me is that I know I'm going there on purpose to try to find some work for us both, and that cramps what little style I've got."

"You've got *tons* of style, and you know it," I said, stroking her bare brown arm. "I know what you mean though. I feel the same when I go. Let's hope the flyers and cards do the trick. If we don't get any response, we'll know that we're up shit creek."

"Then what would we do?"

"Well, persevere for a bit, and if nothing comes up, I guess we'd have to think about moving somewhere else, maybe further south," I said, striving to maintain an upbeat tone of voice.

"But not back home?"

"Well, no, that'd be a real cop-out, wouldn't it?"

"Yes, but our savings won't last forever, and we're not getting much rent from our house," she said, which was true enough, as out of the monthly rental we received we had to use about half of it to pay off our modest mortgage. "If nothing significant comes up by Christmas, I'll have to think about applying for jobs back home for the following school year."

"Really?" I asked, shocked by her decisive tone of voice. "What about a job in a language school somewhere else in Spain?"

"Hmm, on the websites they usually ask for the TEFL qualification, which I haven't got."

"But you're a proper teacher," I said, knowing that the TEFL was a month-long intensive course that practically anyone could take, as long as they could read, write and cough up over a thousand quid.

"Yes, in a big city I'm sure I'd find something, but we don't want that, do we?"

"Not really, no. I'd rather be in Todmorden than a big city anywhere. Still, aren't we being a bit pessimistic? We've only just started looking."

"Yes, you're right, but I'm glad we rented."

"Me too," I said, thinking about Brian and the unsellable house he had no wish to sell. He and his wife had four pensions to play with, but we were getting no nearer to earning ours, another worry that I pushed firmly to the back of my mind.

# 4

We took our card and flyer templates to the printing shop on Manuel Simó Marín Street early the following morning and were able to pick up the four packages late in the afternoon, after which we met Álvaro in the park.

"Is it permitted to put these up in the streets?" Emma asked him in her precise Spanish.

"Not really, but people do. Go out late in the evening and stick some loosely to lampposts, so that people can take them," he said, looking cool and relaxed in his shirt and slacks, and making me feel a bit of a tourist in my t-shirt and shorts, as the evenings were slightly cooler by then. "It would be better to take them to the shops, bars and other places though, and also leave some cards there."

"We'll do that tomorrow," Emma said, before looking at me and tapping our bag of advertising material.

"Give me some sheets and some cards," said Álvaro.

"Oh, how many?" Emma asked.

"Oh, about fifty sheets and a hundred cards."

"Really?" I asked, having understood him perfectly, being a hotshot at numbers by then.

"Yes, I walk around the town every day. One week from now every place that I visit will be advertising the best teacher and builder in town," he said with an especially cheeky grin.

"Oh, that's kind of you, Álvaro. But it's a lot of trouble," said Emma.

"Not at all. I like to visit the shops and other places. There is little crime here, so…" he said, holding both palms in the air.

"Will it not be bad for your job?" I asked very slowly, venturing into the future tense. I pictured Brian's smug face and realised that he hadn't considered either of the Spanish verbs for 'to be' important enough for his definitive list of eight.

"No, a few every day is no problem."

"Some shops might not want to put them up," said Emma.

"Oh, they will, at least for a while. I get on with everybody here, even those I don't like much. A local policeman must be friendly and diplomatic."

"Do you not have… enemies?" I asked.

"Ha, no. Some Ontinyent families dislike each other, but I have only lived here for thirty-five years, so I am still an outsider," he said with a chuckle.

"So we will always be outsiders, I suppose," said Emma.

"Sí, pero viva la diferencia," he said, before grasping her hand across the table and squeezing it. "That you will soon speak good Spanish is the most important thing. Many of the recent foreigners don't try, which is a great pity, especially for them. I cannot imagine living in another country and not speaking the language. I would feel so lost and useless. Before I met Chelo, I was friendly with a girl from Colombia and I went there with her on holiday. A wonderful country and I could live there, but in a place where they don't speak Spanish…" He tutted loudly and waved his finger in the air. "Impossible. The English are very peculiar people. One lady a few weeks ago asked me a question in English and was annoyed because I didn't understand. I told her politely that we were in Spain, but I'm not sure she even understood that. Yes, you are strange, even little Luke here," he said to the returning wanderer.

"Yo no soy extraño, Álvaro," he said like a native, so we were almost as relaxed as he was about his fast-approaching first day at school.

We'd already been to meet his form teacher and she'd said that a bright six-year-old like him would have no problem whatsoever picking up both Spanish and Valenciano in no time. We planned to invite our neighbours Juan and Carmen to a slap-up lunch in order to thank them, and especially their children Claudia and Oscar, for the invaluable language classes they'd inadvertently given our son.

Early the following morning, a Saturday, I cycled into town armed with a few dozen flyers and a roll of sellotape, and I shot around like a bicycle courier, sticking one to every strategic lamppost that I passed. I arrived home at ten and told Emma that I was going out for a proper ride.

"Are you not tired? You could go tomorrow, or just about any other day."

"No, and I'm inspired. I'm going to cycle through a few villages and stick up some more flyers."

"That's a good idea, but we could drive if you wanted."

"No, It'll feel less intrusive just pulling up on my bike and slapping them on."

So, after a bowl of cereals and two cups of tea, I hurtled back into town and took the back road to Agullent, a biggish village about four miles to the east, where I stuck up a dozen flyers, before heading further east to Albaida, which is on the cover of this book and you'll see why later on. I did the same thing there and was even brave enough to stop for a drink in a bar in the corner of the big square and ask the young bloke in charge to stick one up and also to keep hold of a few cards, which he acquiesced to very pleasantly.

Still full of beans, I moved on to Adzeneta d'Albaida, before taking the pretty minor road still further coastward and visiting the hamlets of Carrícola, Otos and Beniatjar, which nestled at the foot of the striking Benicadell mountain and was the most picturesque of them all. Having run out of steam and flyers, I pedalled slowly back along the same road and thought how wonderful it would be to live in that part of the valley, which was more rural and unspoilt than where we were.

"How did it go?" Emma asked when I slumped into my usual chair on the porch, pouring with sweat, but chuffed about the little mission I'd completed.

"It's brilliant further down towards the coast," I said as I took off my helmet, before filling her in on my exploits and discoveries.

"It sounds great, and I do hope someone'll ring about building work."

"And classes."

"Those, too, but I think you're going to be the main breadwinner for a while. There are no grandparents here to look after Luke. Let's drive down there tomorrow and go for a walk. It should be quite cool in the morning, according to the forecast."

So that's what we did, and an epic walk it turned out to be. After a little online research I'd persuaded Emma that if we set off early enough we could conquer the peak of Benicadell, as although it was about eleven hundred metres high – just over a hundred more than Scafell Pike – we'd be starting from quite high up.

"Me and Luke will stick around the lower slopes, I think," she said when I pointed out the peak as we drove towards Albaida.

"It doesn't look so steep from close up, and there's bound to be an easy route up that rocky bit at the top, there always is."

"Me and Luke aren't bothered about conquering peaks, are we, Luke?" she said, pointing up the mountain after we'd parked the car near a Casa Forestal reached by passing Beniatjar and turning right about a mile later, before driving up a fairly smooth track for a couple of miles.

"I want to go to the top," he said.

"That's my boy."

"You'll be carrying him then," Emma said as she applied sun cream to his already tanned face and limbs.

Luke was a tough little lad and after playing outside for hours on end every day, we'd seen that he was becoming a strong walker. We took our time, of course, and it was only after an hour or so that I began to pick him up now and then to give his little legs a rest. Nearing the top, however, I handed Emma our rucksack and carried him almost all the time, as I didn't want him to be too tired to make the descent, and when we stopped for a rest before tackling the last bit to the summit, I think I was the most fatigued member of our party.

"Maybe I'll wait here with Luke," Emma said. "It looks a bit hairy up there."

"I want to go to the top," said you know who.

"You'll have to walk, Luke. It looks too steep for me to carry you," I said.

"Vamos," he said, so we did, and although a health and safety officer might not have approved, I managed to steer and lift him up the final crags to the top.

The view from the peak was wonderful, as not only could we see the whole of the Albaida valley, but also the higher peak of Mount Cabrer to the southwest and the Alicante mountains to the southeast, as well as a long reservoir looking very blue in the sun.

"Wow, it's like having the Lake District on our doorstep," Emma said as she took a few shots.

"Yes, it even beats the view from Stoodley Pike," I said, referring to a monument on the moors above Todmorden. "Do you like it, Luke?" I asked him in Spanish.

"Sí, me gusta mucho."

"Are you glad we came right to the top?" I asked. Emma's reticence about him tackling the last bit was understandable in a way, as the kids at her school in Todmorden all had to wear fluorescent jackets to walk about three hundred yards to the park.

"Yes, but I want to go down now."

After carefully negotiating the tricky top section, we strolled down to the well-preserved ice house – a round structure with a stone dome in which they used to pack snow in order to make ice in the olden days – and stopped to eat our sandwiches. We'd seen a few more people going up or down, but anywhere so beautiful would have been much busier on a fine Sunday in Britain. We still had Montcabrer and the whole of the wooded Sierra de Mariola to explore, so we felt well provided for as far as walking went, though we were soon to find that in lower lying rural areas there were few footpaths and we had to make do with the wider tracks.

We'd managed to spend the whole morning and afternoon without talking about our work prospects, though I'd spotted Emma checking her phone a few times.

"Is there anything else we can do to find work?" she asked as we entered the streets of Ontinyent, which seemed like a heaving metropolis after our day in the country.

"Well, we'll have to keep on with the flyers and cards, and still visit the British bar, and other bars, I guess," I said, as it was to be another year before some enterprising expats started a rastro, or flea market, near the top of the town. "Apart from that we just have to pray that our phones ring. I mean, if no-one calls at all we'll know we've made a big mistake."

"Yes, but someone's bound to ring soon. Is there anything like a job centre here, do you know?"

"I haven't heard of one, but I'll ask Álvaro when I next see him."

As we munched our cured ham and cheese bocadillos outside Álvaro's casita a few mornings later, I remembered to ask him.

"Un centro de trabajo?" he mused. "Not as far as I know. There is a place where people go to claim certain payments if they are not working, but whether you can search for jobs there, I don't know."

"So how do people find jobs?"

"They ask around."

"Vale," I said, meaning 'right'.

"But why do you ask, Sam? Neither you nor Emma need to do work other than teaching and building."

"I hope not, but…" I pointed to my phone. "Nothing yet."

"Don't worry, it is still early, and I haven't finished my propaganda tour. When I leave the sheets and cards I also tell people how wonderful you both are."

"Ha, gracias!"

"But I think it is more likely that they will call about the classes rather than the building work."

"I know. Why use an English builder?"

"Exactly. It was a good idea of yours to visit the villages, as some foreigners live in them and near them," he said, before licking his lips and thinking for a while. "You could also cycle on the country tracks around Ontinyent, looking for their houses."

"How will I know the houses are of foreigners?"

"Hmm, it is difficult. Some have pretty tiles with foreign names, but I suppose if they have done that they have probably completed their reforms."

"I could put up my sheets near the tracks," I said.

"Yes, on the telegraph poles or other places. You mustn't lose heart, Sam," he said, grasping my arm and shaking it about. "Once you do one excellent job, you will get more work."

"And are you sure I can buy a van or a pickup quickly?"

"In an hour. I know them. They will not sell you a bad vehicle," he said with a wicked grin.

"Are they… scared of you?"

"Ha, no, but people are curious beings. They think that because I wear a uniform that I might have special powers or mysterious contacts. It is hacienda they are really scared of."

"Hacienda?"

"Tax. The tax authorities." He rubbed his finger and thumb together. "Here we like to pay little tax. Our favourite money is black, ha ha."

"At first I will not pay the autónomos," I said, referring to the monthly self-employment payments. "First I work a little, then I start to pay."

"Oof! Don't start to pay for a long time. Once you start, you never stop. If you have bad months, like maybe in summer, that is bad luck, you still pay." He punched the palm of his hand several times, to denote repeated payments, I assumed.

"But I don't want to… have problems."

"Hmm, I think your work will be in the countryside, for foreigners. That is less risky than working in a town or village for Spaniards." He did a bit more thinking. "We will get you a van rather than a pickup, I think."

"Pickups are better, for ladders and things," I said, not because it was true, but because I rather fancied owning a big, chunky Nissan rather than another boring Ford Transit or similar.

"Hmm, but a van is more discreet. Listen, when you get a job, I will come with you to see it, then I can advise you what to do."

"If I get a small job, I suppose I will use the car, and maybe tell them my van is being repaired," I said, somehow, because my Spanish was still pretty basic, but I was improving all the time.

"Good." He clapped his hands. "Now you must get some practice, so we will attempt to put those metal beams onto the roof of my fine workshop."

"You need…" I began, before pointing to the building and holding my arm at a slight angle.

"I know. For that we have those blocks and bricks over there. Vamos, I will mix."

I enjoyed doing the brickwork upon which to lay the sloping beams, but when we began to lift them into place the following morning, a new problem occurred to me. Back in Yorkshire I'd sometimes worked solo, but quite often I'd enlisted the help of a semi-retired labourer called Stan, especially when doing jobs that would have been difficult to do alone, like this one. Once we'd got the beams in place – easy work between the two of us – I expressed my concern about lone working to Álvaro.

"Oh, you are a strong man. You would have managed."

"Maybe, but sometimes I need another man, maybe," I said, having become very fond of the word for maybe – quizá or quizás – as it filled many a gap in my lexicon.

"Then you call me," he said, punching his slim but strong chest.

"Thanks, but maybe you at work."

"Oh, Sam, stop worrying! Do all English people worry so much about every little thing?"

"Yes."

"What a strange breed you are." He shook his head. "When that bridge arrives, we will cross it," he said, prompting me to make a mental note of the Spanish version of that very useful saying. "Now, go back to your lovely Emma and little Luke and try to enjoy your free time."

"He starts school today."

"Ha, they will love him and his curly blond hair! He will be a big success, you will see."

# 5

Luke's hair wasn't really blond, just a lighter shade of brown than ours, but he did seem to have made rather a hit during his first day at school, which was on Albaida Avenue in the eastern part of town and had been recommended by Helen because many 'decent' families lived in the newish blocks of flats around there. Though there were several foreign children at the school, he was the only one in his class, and judging from what he told us he'd been the centre of attention during most of the day.

"Did you understand your teacher?" Emma asked him as we made our way towards our double-parked car.

"More or less."

"And the other children?"

"More or less," he said again, giving us both a lesson in the art of not worrying about things needlessly.

"Did you make any friends?" I asked him.

"They all want to be my friend. We'll see," he said enigmatically, so we didn't bombard him with further questions.

Oh, to be so young and carefree! I thought as I turned up the hill to our house after negotiating some heavy traffic, the school run appearing to be as much of an institution there as it is in Britain nowadays, despite the compact nature of the town. I thought about giving Luke flyers and cards to distribute among his classmates, but decided against it, though Emma was obviously thinking more seriously along similar lines.

"The schools would be a good place to put up my flyers," she said. "I should have thought of that before."

"Well, our school awareness has only really started today. I'll nip down on the bike before it goes dark and stick some up."

"We could all come down together."

"No, I prefer the bike," I said, as I'd found that the speedy getaway it enabled me to make got me quickly away from the scene of an action that I still thought a bit cheeky, goodness knows why.

I arrived home on my bike in the failing light, hot and flustered after tearing around the unexpectedly busy streets, having forgotten that many Spaniards finish work at seven or later.

"I've had a call," said Emma as I was locking my rather old road bike up on the porch.

"That was quick," I said, though quite a few people had observed my by now expert flyer-sticking operations with rapt attention.

"No, it was a lady who picked up a card in a bakery, so it must be one that Álvaro left them. She wants me to give her son classes to help him pass English at secondary school. He's sixteen and had to retake his exam in September, so she wants him to pass first time this year."

"Will he come here?"

"No, she wants me to go to their flat in town, two evenings a week."

"Evenings?"

"That's what she said. I think she wants to be around during the classes, as it sounds like he's a lazy sod."

"Lazy sod," echoed a sleepy Luke.

"A lazy boy, I mean. I suggested fifteen euros an hour and she pulled a face."

"How do you know?" I asked, as we didn't have smartphones then.

"Well, I could sort of tell when she said 'vale' and sighed that she was pulling a face, so I said, 'Oh, but of course if it's two classes a week I can do those for twenty-five.' I think that clinched it," she chuckled.

"It's not much, if you have to drive there and back."

"It's a start. I get the impression that other teachers might be cheaper, but I did spell out that I'm a proper schoolteacher."

"Yes, with a bit of luck it'll lead to more students. Well done, love," I said, giving her a sweaty hug and a peck on the cheek.

"I start tomorrow at eight, so you'll have to put Luke to bed."

"No problem," I said, wondering when I'd get my first call.


Emma's first class was money for old rope, she told me on her arrival home at twenty past nine, before popping in to give Luke a goodnight kiss.

"Yes, his mother wants me to explain the textbook to him so he can stay ahead of the rest. He's a nice lad really and it'll be good for me, as I'll get used to using all the Spanish grammatical terms."

"I thought you knew them already."

"I *know* them, but I need to have them on the tip of my tongue," she said, sticking it out to illustrate her point.

"But aren't you supposed to speak English in English class?"

"That's what I thought, but this is more of a cramming class than anything else. I might get quite a few of those, with any luck, as Lourdes, Pepe's mum, told me that from sixteen onwards a lot of students start to struggle to pass English, or maybe she just said that because Pepe isn't the brightest spark," she said, seeming quite enthused by her maiden outing.

"Well, I'm really glad that Pepe looks like being a nice lad to teach. In your absence I've prepared a healthy tuna salad," I said, as we'd got used to eating lunch at twoish and dining lightly at about nine, just like the locals. "And we'll open a bottle of wine to celebrate."

"OK, but it's not time to celebrate just yet," she said as she gave me a hug.

"It's a start."

That night we made love for the first time in well over a week, as I think our first paid work in Spain had de-stressed us enough to allow us to unwind, rather than using our pillow talk time to fret about our lack of progress. After packing in our well-paid jobs only two months earlier, ours was an unusual and disturbing situation to be in, but I think we both slept easier that night after Emma had earned our first twelve-and-a-half euros.

That Saturday Emma got another call, this time to teach a brother and sister of seven and eight, also twice a week.

"This will be different, as they're doing fine at school," she told me when I returned from a flyer-sticking expedition along the lanes and tracks between Ontinyent and Fontanars, a village about twelve miles inland where the Albaida valley opens out onto higher, flatter terrain. I'd seen a lot of posh houses on my travels, so I didn't hold out much hope, but I'd enjoyed the ride more than my poor thin tyres had. I'd buy a mountain bike when I'd earned some money, but not before.

"Where will you do the class?"

"In their flat in town, seven till eight, Mondays and Wednesdays."

"So that's four evening's work then."

"Hmm, yes and no. It's four evenings taken up, but hardly four evenings' work, unless I can squeeze another class in somewhere. When the next person rings I'll suggest classes at four, as most schools finish at three."

The next person rang her the following morning while we were walking back down from the Ermita de San Esteve, a much restored seventeenth century hermitage on the modest mountain range behind our house, about three miles to the northwest of the town. Álvaro had told me that the hillside had been heavily wooded until the terrible forest fires of 1994, and though they had recovered a little, it had become clear that the dense pine woods were never going to grow back.

I heard Emma suggest a four o'clock slot, before seeing her nose wrinkle as she listened to the woman's voice respond. It turned out that little Paco would be far too tired to have classes at that time, and it was only with reluctance that she accepted the quarter to seven slot that Emma then proposed.

"So I guess that's Tuesday and Thursday evenings taken care of," she said as we strolled on hand in hand.

"Yes, so when I start work I won't see much of you on those days, *if* I start work."

She squeezed my hand. "Of course you will. You'll get a call any day now, you'll see. These evening classes are OK for looking after Luke, but they aren't ideal for us, are they?"

"No, that had crossed my mind too."

"You know, I've had a thought; a bit of a crazy thought, but I think I could soon pull it off."

"Striptease?"

"Ha, yes, you'll do striptease and I'll teach Spanish."

"Spanish?" I asked, as I assumed the striptease was a joke, though if the money had been good I'd probably have done it.

"Yes, to the Brits and any other foreigners who want to learn. Not now, but in about six months I reckon I'll be good enough to pull it off. Álvaro says that my accent's quite good, and the few women I've spoken to in the bar haven't got a clue. I mean, *you* could teach them a lot, never mind me."

"Thanks," I said, absorbing the combined compliment and acknowledgment of my inferior language skills quite happily. "Would they want to learn it, though?"

"Oh, I'm sure some do. Those classes could be during the day, you see, which would be better for us."

"Well, it's certainly worth thinking about," I said as I fingered the inert phone in my back pocket. Only Emma and Álvaro had ever rung the damn thing and it was starting to annoy me. Obviously I really was pleased that Emma was getting classes, but each new student was a sort of blow, not exactly to my pride, but… well, as I can't think of another word for it, I guess it was my pride. Back home there'd been months where I'd taken home three grand, not many, but how long would it take me to earn that out here?

"Maybe I should think about giving English classes too," I said when we reached the car.

"You?"

"Why not? I did my A levels, remember. I'm not *just* a dumb builder," I said, as I'd actually won a place at Bradford University, to study History of all things, before I'd got the building bug while labouring for a highly skilled stonemason near Littleborough, just down the road from Todmorden.

"Oh, you could do it easily enough, but it's not your thing. You wouldn't enjoy it, because you'd want to be building."

"True. I think I'll have another look online. If there's a British building company with thirty miles of us I think I'll contact them."

"Hmm, yes, but we'd have to get another car."

"A van, because I wouldn't be working for them forever."

"But you don't want to be travelling too far. You know how tiring it can be."

"Sod that," I snapped, before smiling apologetically. "Sorry, but I need to do something."

"I know, love."

"There'd be one advantage to it too. They do things differently here, like the plastering, so it'd be like a bit of a Spanish apprenticeship for me."

"Have a look when we get back."

While Emma prepared lunch I went online and after a few different searches I came up with about a dozen names and numbers, all of them on or near the coast, in places such as Gandía, Pego, Oliva, Cullera and Ondara, the last two being too far away, but what the hell, I was getting desperate.

"I'll ring them tomorrow," I said as we ate our hake, mash and vegetables.

"You do that, but make thirty miles your limit."

"OK, love."

The only one of them who was remotely interested in the very keen builder based in the back of beyond was a chap called Darren, who lived near Tavernes de la Valldigna, north from Gandía and a mere forty miles away by the main roads. It would take me about an hour to get there, according to google maps, so I hoped that Emma wouldn't be too displeased by my disobedience.

After I'd told Darren all about my varied building experience, instead of cooing with admiration he asked me curtly if I had a van.

"Ye... Yes."

"What sort?"

"A Vauxhall... Opel Combo," I blurted out. "But I might be changing it this week," I added.

"What for?"

"Oh, another of that type."

"Well, that's good," he said in his West Country accent. "I've got two jobs on at the moment, so I might ask you to get on with one of them."

"Great," I said, wondering how to broach the subject of money.

"I can pay you fifteen euros an hour."

"OK," I replied, though it was a little over half what I'd charged back home. "I can start next Monday. I'll have finished a job I'm doing near here by then," I said, needing to buy time to sort out my inexistent vehicle.

"Hmm, fair enough, though you could have started tomorrow."

"Right, well, I'll call you if I get it finished sooner."

"Is there not much doing up there at the moment then?"

Tired of lying, which I wasn't very good at, I decided to say something a little nearer to the truth. "I haven't been living here for long, so I'm still sussing things out."

"Things'll turn up, which is good, because after the two jobs I'm on now I've got sod all lined up."

"Right, well, I'll get cracking on my job and call you as soon as I've finished it," I said, hating to miss a single day's work, real rather than imaginary.

"OK, lad. Bye."

I hung up and called Álvaro.

"Álvaro, I need a van, right now."

"Good. I am busy now but can meet you there in one hour. Do you remember the place I told you?"

"Sí," I said, having already taken a peek at the commercial vehicle garage on the industrial estate which dominates the eastern approach to the town.

"Una hora," he repeated, before hanging up.

Only then did I seek out Emma, who was sweeping the porch. I told her the good tidings from Tavernes de la Valldigna

"Great. You'd better buy a decent van if you're going to be doing so many miles," she said, realising that my eighty mile daily round trip was a *fait accompli*, and she never was one to nag, thank goodness.

"Yes, I can always sell it if things don't work out."

"Things will work out, love. While you're working for him, jobs will turn up around here, you'll see."

"What if something turns up right away?" I asked, before picturing Álvaro's serene face. "Well, when that bridge arrives, I will cross it," I added in Spanish.

"Is that the right way around?"

"Oh, yes," I said proudly, before kissing her, grabbing my wallet and our bank book, and heading into town.

The huge factories that I passed, such as Colortex and Tejidos Reina, looked impressive, but I couldn't help noticing the small number of cars parked outside places that used to employ several hundred people. Maybe some of those who had been laid off had turned to building work, I mused as I left the main road and approached the garage. By the time Álvaro arrived I hoped to have chosen my van, which with a bit of luck I might have on the road before the day was out.

I made a beeline for two white Opel Combos, which was as good a van as any, but what would I tell Darren? That I'd decided not to change my perfectly good van, or that I'd bought another of the same model? That's the trouble with lying; if you don't get much practice you can be easily exposed later. Many builders are skilled practitioners of the art, as I'm sure you know, but I was sure that my innate honesty had helped me prosper in the long run. Yes, I'd built up a good business back home, I was reflecting when a youngish man in overalls approached me.

"Hola, I am waiting for a friend to come and advise me," I said, having rehearsed the phrase earlier.

"Vale," he replied, before turning to go.

"Oh, how many kilometres have these vans done?"

"I'll get the keys," he said over his shoulder.

He returned with two keys, handed them to me, and told me he'd be in the workshop, so I was to be spared the hard sell that I'd braced myself for after all.

By the time Álvaro arrived in a police car I was listening to the engine of the older of the two vans.

"I didn't know you were working," I said as he marched towards me, looking very martial and efficient.

"Yes, but I must make sure that our citizens circulate in the correct vehicle. Now, what have you seen?"

"These two Combos look OK, and the VW Caddy and the two Berlingos over there."

"Has anyone attended you?"

"Yes, a big man in overalls."

"With very short hair?"

"Yes."

"Jose Manuel!" he boomed at the top of his voice.

The man emerged presently and frowned when he saw Álvaro.

"What? Have you come to close us down?" he asked gruffly.

"Yes, because you are the biggest thieves in town," he replied, before shaking the man's grimy hand.

"Your friend here wants a van, no?" he asked him, no longer looking at me.

"Yes, the best small van you have at the best price."

The man took the two keys from me and walked quickly back into the office, before returning and opening one of the Berlingos. He handed me the key without a word and turned to Álvaro.

"Four years old, sixty thousand kilometres, all long trips. This van is new."

"How much?" Álvaro asked.

"For you, seven thousand, for your friend, six."

Álvaro looked at me and I nodded.

"Start it then," he said, so I did.

"As you see, it is new," said the man, making me wonder if there were no words for 'like new' or 'as good as new', though I knew there were.

"Should we go for a drive?" I asked Álvaro.

"If you like, but there is no need. If Jose Manuel sells you a bad van, I will crush his bollocks," he said, which didn't seem to faze Jose Manuel much, though being as tall as me – about five eleven – and built like a tank, he would probably brush off even more serious threats to his person.

"There is a one year warranty," he said, smiling for the first time.

"I would like to buy it today, if possible," I said, waving my wallet in a rather ridiculous way, as if I wanted to assure him that I didn't intend to pay with grapes or olives.

"Come into the office."

"I must go," said Álvaro. "There has been a road accident and I must go back to the scene."

"Oh, but…"

He gave us a jaunty salute and marched back to his car, so I followed Jose Manuel inside to buy a van that I'd driven for ten yards, five forward, and five back. This trust and implied integrity seemed marvellous to me then, and it didn't occur to me that back home I knew a van dealer who I trusted just as much. I guess when nice things happen to you in Spain, you think, 'Oh, what a wonderful country!' while in your home town you just take them for granted.

"That was quick," said Emma when I'd tooted my horn and switched off the engine, less than three hours after leaving home. "Where's our car?"

"Your car now. We'll go and get it before picking Luke up," I said, before telling her about my morning's work. "It's already taxed and I sorted the insurance right there in the office," I added, as an efficient young lady had taken over from Jose Manuel. She'd spoken to me in English, but I hadn't minded as when you deplete your saving by six thousand euros, you don't want any linguistic errors to mess things up. She called the insurance company for me too, which I'd have had to ask Emma to do, as holding an important conversation over the phone was still beyond me.

"It's a nice shade of blue," said Emma.

"Yes, I'm sort of glad it's not white, especially if I'm not working legally."

"Did that Darren say anything about that?"

"No, so I didn't mention it."

# 6

"I know fifteen an hour isn't much, what with paying the bloody autónomos, but things are tight right now," was one of the first things Darren said to me when we met at eight o'clock in the Restaurante Victor on the outskirts of Tavernes de la Valldigna, two days after buying my nifty blue van, whose diesel engine ran like a dream.

"Yes," I replied, sipping my coffee and thinking hard.

"You are paying autónomos, aren't you?" asked the lean, stocky man who I guessed was in his mid-fifties.

"Oh, er... no, I'm not actually," I said sheepishly. "I haven't worked much so far, you see."

"Hmm, well, we'll be out in the country, so I don't suppose it matters for now."

"No," I said, before exhaling slowly through my nose.

"In any case, it'll probably just be these two jobs, as like I said, I haven't got much lined up," he said, his frown crinkling his nut-brown forehead, which was a high one for a builder, though his short grey hair had receded quite a bit. "We'd better do both jobs together though, just in case. We'll park your van out of the way and you can wander off if anyone suspicious comes round, though they never have yet," he said in his pleasant lilting accent, one of my favourites outside of Yorkshire.

"That's great. I'm raring to go."

"Did you get your job done quick, then?"

"Yes, it was just a garden wall," I said, using a fib that I'd prepared while driving down the still quiet road towards Gandía.

As I'd expected, we headed towards the coast, and after following his white Transit van down a lane lined with orange groves, we turned off into a fenced compound containing a bungalow that looked pretty much finished to me. Darren jumped nimbly down from his van and told me to park behind an irregular row of cypress trees separating the gravelled area from yet more orange trees. On returning I saw that he'd begun to build a raised porch onto the back of the house and my fingers tingled at the thought of getting stuck in.

"We're to finish that, before building a roof over it to match the rest of the house."

"You've done quite a bit already," I said, pointing to the partly finished breeze-block structure.

"*I* haven't. We're starting today."

"How come?"

"A Spanish company started it. They did a few days and then shot off somewhere else. The owners, a Dutch couple who are away now, got fed up of waiting and sacked them. I reckon they landed a tiling job on one of the big builds on the coast or something like that. There's good money in that; piece work, you know."

"Do you do that sort of thing?"

"No, that'd be a last resort for me. I'd rather do a proper job of work, out of town if possible."

"Yes, it'll be nice working here," I said, shielding my eyes from the sun.

As we had to finish the metre-high breeze-block platform, I started mixing like a man possessed, in order to have time to lay a few blocks alongside Darren before mixing the next load of cement. Though I'd be mainly labouring that day, I wanted him to see my deft trowel hand in action, and by the time we stopped for a break at about half ten, I think he was suitably impressed.

"You're a better worker than I expected," he said as he handed me the large bottle of water.

"Well, I am time served, and I've worked for myself for the last eleven years."

"Time served? Me too. We're a rare breed among British builders out here," he said, his throaty laugh revealing his slightly yellowed teeth.

"Really?"

"Oh, there's a good few of us, I suppose, but there's a lot more who've sort of reinvented themselves out here. I guess at the end of the day it's practical work, so anyone who's handy can pick it up, but they don't have the background that we have, so when they take on big jobs that need a bit of planning, well…" he shrugged and left the sentence unfinished, though that was the longest speech he'd uttered so far, due perhaps to me having proven myself to be a bona fide comrade-in-tools.

"I've got a lot to learn though. I know the plastering is different."

"The yeso, yes, tricky stuff, but you'll soon get the hang of it."

I'll pause for breath here, I think, and reel in my builder's brain a bit, or before I know it I'll be talking you through every job I do from beginning to end, resulting in this sort of occurrence:

*'What happened to that last book you were reading, dear?' someone will ask their partner.*

*'Oh, that one. Well, it started off all right, but then he started going on and on and on about bricks and blocks and trowels and tiles. So boring! Take it to the charity shop if you want.'*

So, to avoid that unfortunate scenario, I shall describe my work only in broad strokes, like when you're applying yeso. Besides, there are loads of decent videos on YouTube these days about Spanish building techniques, though there weren't nearly so many back in the autumn of 2007.

"You'd better slow down as it's getting hot now," Darren said at about midday.

"Ha, yes, I'll pace myself a bit. I'm chuffed to be working again."

"So was that garden wall not work?"

"Er, that was bullshit, I'm afraid. I didn't have a van, you see, so I had to get one quick. Sorry about that."

"Ha, I sort of guessed as much, but I can see you're a good lad. I told you a little fib too."

"Oh."

"About not having work lined up. I've got plenty, but I had to see how you worked first."

"Right," I said, before this outbreak of honesty made me reckless. "I'm sure I'll enjoy working for you, Darren, but it's a long drive every day. I hope I'll get work over my way soon, but until then I'll come every day that you need me."

"Of course, like I said on the phone, things'll turn up. It took me a good year to get going."

"How long have you been in Spain?"

"Twelve years now, the best of my life," he said with a grin.

"Will you be retiring any time soon?"

"Me? No, I wouldn't know what to do with myself all day. When I slow down I'll do less, that's all."

"Sounds like the best plan."

Then we hugged and kissed each other on both cheeks, before cutting our palms and becoming blood brothers forever. Well, we didn't go that far, but it was good to have cleared the air sooner rather than later, as I could see that he was as straight a bloke as I liked to think I was, and still am.

I arrived home at eight o'clock feeling very, very tired.

"You look done in," said Emma as she took my knapsack from me and gave me a kiss.

"I am, but it's been good," I said, before traipsing back to the house, opening a beer, and telling her all about my first day's work in Spain.

"We'll be doing nine-hour days, so it'll be worth my while driving down there," I concluded.

"He sounds like a nice chap, and it's good that you've talked to him straight. You always were a rotten liar."

"Yes, you know, he reminds me of Walter a bit," I said, referring to the stonemason who had given me the building bug, rather like Tim and Sue had passed on the Spanish one. I'd gone on to serve my slightly belated apprenticeship with him and we were still in touch, though he'd retired by then. He hadn't been very impressed when I'd told him about our move to Spain.

"Pah! You'll end up slapping bricks together on blocks of flats fert tourists."

"I hope not, Walter."

"You'll not get as much chance to work wi' stone as round here, any road," he'd said, and I hadn't forgotten.

"Is he a stonemason too?" Emma asked, snapping me out of my reverie.

"Who? Oh, Darren. Not like Walter, but he uses it when the customer'll cough up for it. We'll be doing a bit of stone cladding on the porch pillars, so that's something. No class tonight?" I asked, suddenly realising that she shouldn't be there.

"I moved it forward half an hour and took Luke round to Juan and Carmen's. We just got back five minutes ago." She pointed at Luke, who was ploughing his little bike along the gravel in the fading light.

"Shit, I forgot all about your classes. What'll we do? I'll have to finish earlier."

"No, no, your work comes first right now. I'm going to have to tell Pepe's mum that I can't do eight till nine. I'll offer them two hours on Saturday mornings, and I don't think my seven till eight classes will be a problem, as Carmen doesn't mind Luke playing round there for a while."

"It's going to be a logistical nightmare," I said, before opening another beer.

She ruffled my sweaty hair. "No it's not. Do you know what I'm going to do?"

"Go on."

"Anyone who rings from now on will be offered classes anytime between nine and three."

"That won't suit them."

"I know, but what can I do? If you carry on with Darren, I think I might bring forward my Spanish class idea. Those people are free all day long, so morning classes should suit them."

"You think of everything," I said, lurching towards her with open arms.

"Go and have a shower while I make dinner," she said, smiling and backing away.

After two more days of slightly less frantic work, Darren and I had completed the porch structure by Friday evening.

"I'll be coming with the concrete truck blokes tomorrow, so we'll be doing the pillars and beams next week," he told me as we were washing up.

"Great, I'll be well rested by then," I said, as working in the September heat had taken it out of me, though my tan was coming along nicely.

"Here you are." He handed me a wad of notes which I thanked him for and slipped into my pocket.

"Count it, you pillock," he laughed.

I did and it came to four hundred euros. "You can't imagine how it feels to be earning money again, Darren."

"Oh, I can. I ought to pay you a bit less, as you're not paying autónomos, but what the hell, you'll be paying them soon enough, worse luck. I still owe you five euros, but I think we'll nip out for dinner one day next week, so that'll be your contribution. Have a good rest and we'll meet in the bar on Monday at eight. We'd better put in a day on the other job or the same thing'll happen to us as happened to the Spanish who were working here."

"Bye, Darren, and thanks again."

As it turned out, that weekend I was going to get a taste of things to come. After dinner I called Álvaro to see what he was up to, and his reply sent shivers through my weary limbs.

"Ha, just the man I wanted to speak to! Tomorrow you are invited to eat a tasty fideuà which Chelo will prepare."

"Great, what time shall we come? Emma has a class from ten till twelve."

"Then Emma can come after that. I request you, however, to arrive at nine."

"Oh, why?"

"Because you are going to help me to finish my workshop roof."

"Oh… fine," I said, pulling a rather pained face.

"You don't sound enthused by the idea, Sam."

"Oh, I am. I am a little tired now, that is all."

"Ah, how has you work gone?"

"Well, very well. See you at nine tomorrow."

"Vale, ciao."

In the event, lifting and securing the grey corrugated roof panels onto the metal beams wasn't too onerous, as Álvaro had everything ready and had already drilled the beams. It was a job for two, that was all, or I doubt he would have required my presence. Luke played happily on and around the vegetable plot, and when Emma arrived from her rescheduled class she joined Chelo and learnt how to make fideuà, a seafood pasta dish made in a paella pan.

We talked about all sorts of things over lunch, including Chelo's work as a mortgage adviser in a bank. She thought that people were overstretching themselves financially in order to buy their dream homes, something she didn't approve of, but was obliged to encourage.

"It is the same in Britain," Emma said. "Sometimes the mortgage is above the value of the house."

"I foresee disastrous consequences," said Chelo.

"When?" I asked, as from a professional point of view I was keen for the housing boom to go on forever. New builds weren't likely to affect me much, but the money always filters down and benefits smaller builders like Darren, and hopefully me.

"Oh, who knows? Three years, two years, maybe less, but it cannot go on. Everywhere they are building like crazy, both in the towns and on the coast. There is much speculation and I have persuaded Álvaro not to buy a property near the beach just because his optimistic colleagues are doing so."

I'd heard very similar words from Álvaro's mouth, during our first meeting in the park when Chelo had taken a backseat, so to speak, and I smiled at him on remembering his wise words.

"Yes, Chelo has convinced me to be cautious. Two of my colleagues have already bought apartments and are taking out mortgages to buy another. They are going to rent them out and retire early."

"They think they are," said Chelo, shaking her head, before asking Luke how he was enjoying school.

"I like it."

"Have you made many friends?"

"Oh, yes," he said, before rushing off to play with the wheelbarrow, perhaps unwilling to share his secrets with irrelevant adults. He hadn't told us much either, but it was clear that he was thoroughly enjoying himself and that the rapidly falling language barrier wasn't an issue for him. He had already said a few Valencian words at home, such as molt bé instead of muy bien, though this hadn't happened previously when he'd only played with Claudia and Oscar, our neighbours' children. I asked Álvaro why he though this might be.

"Let me see, Juan and Carmen, ah, Juan has a blue BMW, no?"

"Yes."

"Hmm, they are, or think they are, of the social elite of Ontinyent, so they prefer not to speak Valenciano, as it is considered to be the vulgar language of the peasant."

"And is it?" Emma asked.

"In a way, certainly during Franco's time, when it was prohibited, though people spoke it, of course, unless they were doing official business. For years now there has been a great revival, but Castellano is still the most important language to learn. We must look outwards, not inwards. Isn't that so, Chelo?"

"Totally. Valenciano is for domestic use only," she said with a chuckle. "It is practically the same as Catalan, but most of us are not so fanatical about it as they are. They don't feel Spanish, but we do."

"Do you think Sam and I should learn it?" Emma asked her, causing me to cross my fingers.

"No, well, first perfect your Castellano, then, if you feel like it, learn it. It will please local people, but I think they will still answer you in Castellano, as it is synonymous with people from elsewhere."

"Salut, i força al canut," said Álvaro, raising his glass.

"Salut!" we replied, before clinking our glasses of white wine and drinking.

"Isn't canut a… vulgar thing?" Emma asked him.

"No." he raised his index finger as he often did before delivering interesting or astounding news. "The canut is not the male member as is supposed, but a kind of purse which used to be made from the skin of the bull's scrotum."

"Ugh," said Emma.

"So, it does not mean 'force to your… thing,' but 'force to your purse', which is a very Catalan sentiment, as they are so mean that they don't stop in the sun so as not to give shade."

Neither Emma nor I got that one. It was too fast for me, and though Emma caught the words, she wasn't sure if she was supposed to laugh or not. To this day I find Spanish humour a bit basic, but I laughed politely when Emma translated it for me. I then broached a subject that had been bothering me for a while, namely whether or not to start paying autónomos. As Chelo was probably pretty clued up about such things, I looked at her when I spoke.

"Hmm, the autónomos payments are a great burden for many self-employed people, unless their business is quite large. You will have to pay about two hundred euros every month for social security, as well as paying tax on your declared earnings. You must also pay an assessor a monthly fee to help you with the paperwork," she said, very slowly and clearly.

"Vale," I said, bracing myself for her final verdict.

"I think that when you know you are going to earn at least €1500 every month, continuously, you should start to pay, though it also depends how… conspicuous your work activities are. Also remember that you still have to pay during the holidays. This seems obvious, but sometimes people don't take this into account. When self-employed people come to me for mortgage advice, I urge them to be cautious, despite what my boss tells me to do."

"Right, I will think about it," I said, already thinking hard. Fifteen euros an hour cash in hand amounted to a good deal of money after a full week's work, and had I been sure I was going to carry on working for Darren indefinitely I'd have felt obliged to start paying, partly on moral grounds, but mostly because it wouldn't be fair on him to have to risk being caught with an illegal worker on his hands. After just three days' work, however, I knew that being away from home for up to thirteen hours a day wasn't sustainable, not if I wanted to have any sort of family life, so I decided to take each week as it came and put money aside for the rainy days that might arrive at some point.

"Nor are self-employed people able to claim unemployment benefits, which seems very unfair," Chelo said when she judged that my brain had ceased whirring. "If I were you I would wait for a while."

"And always park your van in a discreet place," Álvaro said, raising his finger. "Anyway, now that my workshop is practically finished, I will allow you to rest at the weekends," he added, before grasping my thigh hard, as he was wont to do from time to time.

# 7

Do you remember what I said about getting a taste of things to come? Well, that following week Darren and I finished tiling a bathroom in a plush apartment in Cullera on the Monday, before spending the rest of the week at the bungalow, erecting four pillars and attaching some of the wooden beams. While we were having lunch in Xeraco on Friday, I received a call and stepped outside to answer it. On returning inside, Darren saw my ruffled brow and raised his eyebrows in an interrogatory way.

"Someone who wants me to do a job," I said, scratching my head.

"Great, go for it."

"Hmm, it's not much, just a partition wall in a casita somewhere near Albaida. The bloke's even got all the beams, plasterboard and stuff ready, but his wife won't let him do it. He says she says he'll make a mess of it, and she saw one of my flyers."

"Hmm, more of a carpentry job than anything, but of course you'll have to skim the plasterboard. Hopefully he'll have bought yeso retardado, which is easier to use. If not, get some of that. A couple of day's work, if that, as I'm guessing he'll already have cut the beams, hopefully to the right size," he said with a chuckle, obviously visualising the job that might take his worker away at a time when he would need him, up on the porch roof.

"I've told him I'll call round tomorrow morning. If the price is right I might even make a start and then finish it next Saturday," I said, as I'd only worked on Sunday a handful of times in my life.

"Take Monday off, if you like. I'll do a bit more tiling in the apartment."

"No, it's nothing of a job and Emma works on Saturday mornings anyway," I said, before remembering Luke. It's not that I lacked awareness of our lovely son, but back home we had never, ever had to worry about childcare, as my parents were available 24/7, literally. "Yes, I'll be here on Monday."

"We'll meet at the apartment in Cullera anyway, in case you change your mind."

"I won't," I said, as a man who only a week earlier had no work at all doesn't throw €135 away lightly.

As Juan and Carmen, the presumed snobs, were happy to have Luke round at theirs on Saturday morning, I didn't have to take him to Albaida after all, where I'd arranged to meet my prospective customer in the bar in the corner of the square at nine o'clock. Despite feeling a bit fatigued, I was still quite excited about my first solo job, but not half as keen as I'd have been if I hadn't been working for Darren.

The man, called Arnaud, was a plump Belgian of about sixty who spoke pretty good English, and after a quick coffee I followed his shiny Land Cruiser out of town and onto a lane beyond Adzeneta d'Albaida, another biggish village. After climbing a steep track through olive groves, we turned into the gravelled grounds of an impressive two-storey chalet, complete with a triple garage and a large swimming pool, already covered for the winter. His wife, Emilie, proved to be a shadowy figure who I didn't see much of during the next two days.

Yes, the next two days, because on seeing that Arnaud had everything lined up for the job, including the tools, I agreed on his proposed price of €300 and set to work right away, the task being to divide their huge living room into a large and a smaller room, into which separate doors already existed. The price seemed pretty good, though I'd have charged more back home, but the fact that Arnaud insisted on helping me, fairly competently, meant that I sped along at a terrific rate. I mean, it was a bit like Blue Peter, the way he had everything on hand, and I almost expected the double-sided sticky tape to come out at some point.

I think he enjoyed my company as he insisted on inviting me to lunch at a roadside bar in El Palomar, a small village a mile to the north of Adzaneta, where the warm welcome he received made me bold enough to leave a few of my cards. Arnaud and his wife divided their time between Spain and Belgium, and I noticed that his Spanish was passable; better than mine, but not brilliant. I liked the cheerful chap, though he insisted on talking shop throughout the meal – him being a keen, mostly armchair builder – but I didn't mind this as I rather hoped that he'd put in a good word for me among the other expats in an area that I'd already identified as being a desirable one.

I knocked off at about six and arrived home before half past. When I told Emma that I'd be finishing the job the following day she smiled in a way that failed to conceal her annoyance, me being such a perceptive chap.

"It's just a one-off, love. The sooner I finish it, the sooner he can start telling folk what a great builder I am," I said, hoping that my application of the yeso retardado that he had indeed bought wouldn't show me up as the yeso rookie that I was, though the job couldn't have been an easier one to test myself out on.

"You'll be tired on Monday."

"Nah, and I should be done fairly early tomorrow. Three hundred smackers aren't to be sniffed at," I said, my illegal earnings seeming astronomical to me then.

The next day I arrived home at seven, the yeso and a few other bits and pieces having kept me there longer than I'd expected, but Arnaud had paid up happily and promised to put a good word in for me.

"I know several of your monolingual countrymen," he'd said to me during our second quickish lunch in the bar. "So I will recommend you to them."

"Thanks," I said, before lifting my glass of red wine and lemonade. "Salut, i força al canut."

"Ha, molt bé, Sam." We clinked glasses. "You are an example to the others, as many fail to see the advantages of learning the language," he said, before turning to chat to the owner, as if to illustrate his point.

The following week I was hyper-conscious of the phone in my pocket, as I expected it to ring at some point and provide me with another weekend of work. It didn't, so after another satisfying week's toil with Darren I drove home with slightly mixed feelings, happy to have time to spend with Emma and Luke, but worried that Arnaud's job might have been a flash in the pan.

"Boy, am I looking forward to a quiet weekend," I said as I sipped my customary homecoming beer.

"Right, yes…"

"Am I not to have one, love?"

"Yes, apart from the lunch I've invited Carmen and Juan to tomorrow."

"Oh, that'll be nice," I said with as much conviction as I could muster.

"Hmm, I hope so, though she still speaks to me in English. Anyway, I mentioned them coming to lunch sometime and she seemed ever so keen, so I suggested tomorrow. I'm grateful to them for looking after Luke and at least we'll get it over with. I've bought a paella pan and one of those gas rings and I'm going to make a fideuà."

"Not a paella?"

"No, I'll try one of those when it's just the three of us. I think less can go wrong with pasta than rice. I've bought lots of other bits too, so at least it's given me something to do."

"Have you been bored, love?"

"Well, a bit, when Luke's at school."

"Hmm, it's not ideal, is it?"

"No, but we have to adapt to circumstances. I've had two more calls about classes and one of the women got a bit annoyed when I said I could only do between nine and three. She sort of questioned why I'd put the flyers up, so I've taken a lot of them down."

"Have you?"

"Yes, before I picked up Luke today. Look at this." She handed me a printed sheet.

"Spanish classes in and around Ontinyent," I read, plus a few more details. "It sounds good. I'll nip out and put some up tomorrow morning."

"Don't be daft. I've got all the time in the world to do that. My only worry is that someone might want classes whose Spanish is better than mine. You know, someone who wants to perfect their grammar and stuff."

"I can't see that happening somehow, but when that bridge arrives you can cross it." Emma failed to see the drollery of my word order, so I grasped her hands. "Don't worry about it. Álvaro says that we British worry too much. Things could be a lot worse, like if Darren hadn't taken me on."

"I know," she said, squeezing my hands and looking at them. "Clean your nails when you have a shower."

"Daddy's dirty hands like before," said Luke, who had been doing a puzzle.

"Ay, where there's muck there's brass, m'lad," I said in my strongest Yorkshire accent.

"Cómo?" he asked, maybe thinking that another new language had been introduced.

"Where there is... dirt, there is money," I said in Spanish.

"Vale."

"You know, we oughtn't to speak to him in Spanish," said Emma.

"Oh, why not?"

"Well, though it's great for us, at the moment we're the only people he speaks English to."

"True. We're not seeing much of our fellow expats, are we?"

"No, I might pop into the bar with him after school the odd day, to try to drum up a bit of trade, and meet new people, of course."

"Yes, I think you'll enjoy doing Spanish classes."

"Vive la France."

"Eh?"

"If I hadn't learnt French I'd still be speaking Spanish as bad as you."

"Aw!"

"I'm joking. You're doing *much* better than I expected."

"Hmm, I'll take that as a compliment," I said before drawing her towards me. She was too strong for my enfeebled arms, so I went for my much needed shower.

I don't think I'll give you a blow-by-blow account of our lunch with Carmen, Juan, Claudia and Oscar, as it's still a little excruciating to recall. It might seem petty, but when you're trying your hardest to learn a language only to have every question or comment answered in English, it ends up getting on your wick. I mean, it seemed perfectly clear to me that Emma's Spanish was pretty damn good by then, and I think mine was just about understandable too.

We gave up after a while and tried to be as polite as possible, but I honestly think that if they hadn't been so good about Luke being round there all the time – which delighted the kids, by the way – we'd have all but severed relations with them. To this day I don't know if they were oblivious to what Emma considered a tremendous *faux pas*, or if they were just so dense that they didn't twig. Álvaro's words sprang to mind when Juan told us that he was a great festero, and he did seem to fit the profile of the typical 'Ontinyentino' that our friend had outlined. He worked all hours at a company near Xátiva and seemed a bit materialistic, to say the least, though I could hardly talk at that moment in time, what with my insatiable lust for filthy lucre.

"You should have told us you were taking part in the fiestas, Juan," Emma said when we'd finished her very palatable fideuà.

"Oh, I not think you interesting in fiestas. Outside people not understand it," he replied, which just about sums up the great oaf, as the fiestas had begun in 1860 and I doubt that their shiny, elegant costumes had much similarity to those of the armies that had battled it out many centuries earlier, not to mention the brass bands and cigars.

As I sipped my coffee and tried not to look at my watch, Emma became a little mischievous, maybe due to the fine Valdepeñas white wine she'd drunk, as no expense had been spared for our illustrious guests. While still responding to Carmen's mediocre and Juan's execrable English in English, she began speaking to their children in Spanish, who of course responded like the polite kids they were. She'd speak to Claudia or Oscar for quite a while, before turning to their parents and switching to English, but even this, believe it or not, didn't disturb their equanimity.

When Emma ventured a question to Claudia in Valenciano, however, Carmen's smile became very rigid indeed.

"Er, we don't speak to them in that language, Emma."

"Really?"

"No, they learn it at school and that is sufficient. Juan and I are Castellano speakers, and so are our childrens (sic)."

Whether this premeditated gaffe caused them to refuse Emma's offer of cava or not, I don't know, but we both sighed with relief when they'd left, Claudia insisting that Luke go along with them for a while.

"Well, that's done and dusted," I said, opening the cava anyway.

"Yes, I've got a feeling these get-togethers might not become a regular occurrence. I don't think we're quite the right sort of people."

"Suits me, as long as they'll still have Luke round."

"Their kids love him, and so does Carmen, but if she starts speaking English to him I'll strangle her."

"Estrangular. Yo... la estrangularé."

"Yo, *le* estrangularé. It's an indirect object pronoun."

"What's that when it's at home?"

"Don't worry about it. Luke doesn't, and you'll get there too, eventually.

"Álvaro never corrects me," I said by way of an excuse.

"And why should he? Just listen to him, and the telly, and it'll come."

After a relaxing walk in the Sierra de Mariola on Sunday, where the cooler weather enabled us to enjoy our first picnic lunch, I returned to work on Monday feeling so refreshed that I almost preferred no-one to ring me about a local job. I was getting used to the travelling by then, and the work too, which was much easier in temperatures of less than twenty-five degrees and falling, so on Thursday evening I ran a bold idea past Emma, indirectly at first.

"I think Darren'll always have plenty of work."

"That's good," she said, turning down the sound on the TV.

"Yes, he turns down some jobs. He likes to be in the country, like me, so he prefers doing renovations and pools in the casitas," I said, having started my first ever tiling job on a pool that very day, which was proving to be a piece of cake thanks to Darren's helpful pointers.

"What are you getting at?"

"Oh, nothing."

"Out with it."

"Well, it's just a thought, but I guess there'd be nothing to stop us moving down that way, would there?"

"Yes."

"What?"

"Luke's school, my classes, our friendship with Álvaro and Chelo, and our lease, for a start."

"Hmm, true."

"No, I see your point, but we can't chop and change like that just on a whim."

"A whim that's paying me six hundred-and-odd euros a week."

"Yes, because you're not declaring it yet."

"No, I guess I'll have to look into this autónomos business soon. Maybe you're right, love, but never say never. We'll have to see how we're doing by next summer."

"Yes, but a lot of bridges will go over the water before then."

"Is that how they say it in Spanish?"

"Ha, no, it's a joke, but let's not talk about moving for a while. I'm still trying to get settled here."

"Righto, love," I said, before we snuggled up to watch an American film in Spanish, complete with the unbelievably long advert breaks, but it was all good practice.

# 8

After two days' work on the swimming pool at a chalet near Xeresa, Darren decided that we'd better put in another day at the apartment in Cullera, as the English owners were due to arrive soon and they'd expect to see the work finished. I had just plastered a wall – which Darren could have done faster, but he wanted me to get up to speed – and we were about to wash up and leave when I noticed him looking down from the living room window.

"Anything going on down there?" I asked, as I was keen to get going.

"There's a red car that a bloke's been sat in for the last two hours."

"Really? How do you know?"

"Oh, I like to keep an eye on things. He might be watching us, waiting to see who's going to come out and get in my van."

"Well, I'll be getting in mine," I said, suddenly realising the grave implications of his words, and all because I hadn't got round to going legal.

"Even so, if you don't mind I'd like you to stay here for a bit. I think when I drive off, he'll do the same, so just stick around till he's gone."

"OK."

"I mean, if he's still there in half an hour, go anyway, but we'd better be on the safe side."

"I'll stay till he's gone, and I'll sort out my autónomos as soon as I can."

"It might be best," he said, having clearly been vigilant all along, while I'd been happily pocketing my tax-free wages. He then looked at me and at my work bag. "Why don't you put that clean t-shirt on and I'll take your bag? Then if he doesn't go, you can slip out and won't look too much like you've been working."

I looked down at my stained shorts. "We'll do that, but I'm not going till he's gone. I've been a bit blasé about the whole thing."

"No, but it is time. The work's there, so don't worry about that."

When he'd gone I peered obliquely out of the third-floor window and, sure enough, the red car soon departed. I stuck around for twenty minutes anyway, in case it was a ruse, before locking up and leaving, still feeling a bit nervous as I strolled nonchalantly to my van.

"Where's your bag?" Emma asked me when I arrived home at about twenty past eight, having hit the rush hour traffic.

I explained what had happened. "We're back in the country tomorrow, but on Friday I'd better take the day off and get my autónomos sorted. I should have done it before."

"It hasn't been that long, really, but I suppose now's the time. I'll go to the gestoría that Álvaro recommended tomorrow morning and see how much of it I can sort out," she said, the gestoría being the place where they deal with all kinds of bureaucratic paperwork on behalf of companies and individuals.

"Thanks, love."

"And I'll do your accounts."

"Thanks. No Spanish classes yet?"

"A lady called Caroline who I met in the bar is interested. She's going to talk to a couple of friends, so I might be doing classes with three of them."

"That's great, though I guess three separate classes would be better."

"Hmm, not really, because I think her idea is to make it a bit of a social event. Besides, if all three do decide to come, I can charge twenty euros an hour and it'll still be cheap for them. Caroline's nice, so I expect her friends will be too."

"That's brilliant," I said, grasping her shoulders with my already spotless hands, as apart from my dirty shorts I'd left the apartment in an impeccable state, even rinsing the dust from my steel-toe-capped shoes. "More classes will come soon, once they see how good you are. Oh, what's her Spanish like?"

"Very basic, fortunately. Her and her husband have been here for about two years and she's realised that Spanish isn't just going to sink in as she thought it might."

"Not in that bar, it won't."

"No."

"What about the husband, or husbands? Are they not interested in learning?"

"It doesn't sound like Caroline's is. She says he leaves that sort of thing to her."

"What, speaking?"

"He's a golfer," she said, as if that explained everything, which I suppose it did in a way. The drive to the course – there were none near Ontinyent – the game, the nineteenth hole, the drive back, the rest of the day at home recovering; not an ideal schedule for linguistic integration.

The following day while I worked happily under the benign autumn sun, Emma spent an hour in the gestoría and the rest of the day studying the paperwork she'd received. She'd brought me a few forms to sign and the rather laidback man who had attended her had requested that I show my face at some point and sign a couple more.

"He was quite candid, especially after I told him we were friends of Álvaro," Emma said after I'd read Luke a bedtime story and kissed him goodnight. "I told him how much you were earning at the moment, and he told me how much you should declare."

"How much?"

"Oh, a little over half of it."

"Is that all?"

"Yes, no-one declares anywhere near their full earnings, it seems. I guess that's why they make you pay two hundred a month, to make sure they get something out of you. We'll be paying the gestoría about thirty a month too, and you'll have to bill Darren for at least twenty-five hours a week. There's tax to pay every three months, IVA and IRPF, but against that there's the cost of the van."

"But I bought it before I started."

"I told him that, but he's friendly with the garage owner, as he goes there too, and he thinks he'll be able to get another receipt off him."

"It's a lot to take in," I said, already feeling sleepy.

"I'll explain things to you as we go along. The important thing is that as of next Monday you'll no longer be one of those awful people who don't pay tax."

"Yes, I'll proudly park my van next to Darren's. It's a lot easier in England, and if you don't earn much, you pay hardly anything," I said, though I'd always been lucky enough to have plenty of work.

"Yes, if your work dries up, for any reason, we'll just have to take you off it for a while, which means more paperwork, but that's the way things are here. Still, while you're just working for Darren it'll be fairly simple."

"Yes, and no-one's called since Arnaud. Perhaps the yeso fell off the wall and he told everyone how crap I was."

"It won't have, and someone'll call soon."

It's not that Emma's an oracle, but I wasn't altogether surprised when my phone rang the following afternoon as we were laying the stone coping around the pool. The caller was an English bloke who said he had rather a big job for me at his casita on the outskirts of Ráfol de Salem, a village a few miles beyond Carrícola, the last place I'd visited on my first flyer-posting cycle tour, but which I could reach more quickly by taking the main Albaida to Gandía road. Rather than asking for details on the phone, I agreed to visit him on Saturday morning, but I pointed out that I was quite busy and wouldn't be able to start right away. Us builders are fond of saying that, though if we fear competition we usually get our skates on. He sounded like a potentially awkward type on the phone, my sixth sense told me, but I decided to reserve judgement until I'd met him and seen what he wanted me to do, and for how much.

Ráfol de Salem is a small village and as there wasn't a bar there at the time, I met Barry outside the chemist's shop at ten o'clock, with Luke for company, as Emma was doing her class with young Juan, who wasn't too happy about their new slot, but as he was still behind at school he had little choice in the matter.

"This your apprentice?" Barry asked, viewing my son sceptically through his thick glasses.

"No, he's just come along for the ride," I said to the bald, tanned, scrawny chap who I guessed was about seventy. As there was no coffee to be had, we jumped into the van and followed his battered Citroen Saxo out of the village to his extremely shabby casita.

"What do you want doing?" I asked, though I was tempted to suggest him pulling it down and starting again.

"I want it tarting up," he said in his flat midlands accent, him being from Derby, I later discovered. "A local bloke built it, bit by bit, so I don't think it's as solid as it should be, though I suppose that can't be helped now."

"I wonder what the foundations are like," I said, having noticed a worrying diagonal crack down one of the side walls. Álvaro had told me that his father had laid the foundations of their casita himself, but had used plenty of old metal to strengthen them, so I hoped the builder of this place had done the same, as the last thing I wanted to do was to render the walls, only to have them crack again in a few months' time, but I see that I'm in danger of going into great, unnecessary detail, so I'll cut to the chase.

While Luke entertained himself with Barry's friendly mongrel dog, he showed me around the low-ceilinged, six-room house and pointed out the jobs he wanted me to do. It was what we call in the trade a money pit, and we're more than glad to work on them if the owners are prepared to cough up, but judging by the state of the house and his car, Barry wasn't exactly rolling in it. After we'd completed our tour I spoke frankly to him.

"I'm not sure how sound it is structurally, Barry. I can render the walls and do everything else you want me to do, but I can't promise what the place'll be like a couple of years from now," I said, pointing to the jagged fissure as a prime example of my fears.

"Well, I just want to make it a bit more presentable. I've been badly, you see, and I've realised I'm not going to live forever, so I'd better start spending some of my money," he said with a wheezy chuckle. "Glass of wine?"

"Please."

I ended up spending the best part of two hours there, and as Luke and I drove home I'd come to the conclusion that what Barry wanted, as much as the work, was a bit of company. He'd been suffering from cancer and had suddenly realised how alone he was in the world, as he'd never married and rarely spoke to his sister, who had conspicuously failed to rally round when he'd needed her, though the village folk had been brilliant about driving him to hospital for his treatment and generally looking after him. He'd been given the all-clear but was a changed man, he told me, and had decided to do up his house and go on more trips around Spain.

After a while he started calling me 'duck', which I'd never heard before, and at first I feared that it might mean the same as 'ducky', though he didn't seem to have any designs on me. We were the best of pals by the time we left, but I was glad that on my next visit I'd be able to work as we talked, as though I liked the bloke I didn't think Emma would approve of me spending my Saturdays with him rather than her. Luke and Figo, the dog, had got on like a house on fire too, so at least I'd be able to take him along and give Emma a few hours' downtime.

"I'm a legit builder, by the way, so I can give you proper bills," I'd told him.

"Oh, I'm not bothered about that, duck. I'll pay you in cash, no questions asked, and I'll get the stuff you need, don't worry. It'll give me summat to do."

So, like Arnaud, Barry was going to spare me the trips to the builders' merchant, something I'd have struggled to fit in during the week. When I parked up and Luke ran off to find his mum, I looked at my plain blue van and wondered about getting some logos, and if so, what to put. I fancied 'Construcciones Sam Haigh', or maybe something else with construcciones in it, but as I thought it highly unlikely that I'd get any Spanish customers, I reasoned that something in English would be more appropriate.

"Yes, it's a lovely van," Emma said with a grin as she approached me with a bottle of beer. I told her why I appeared to be mesmerised by my vehicle. "How about 'Sam Haigh, British Builder', or 'Sam Haigh...' oh, nothing rhymes with Haigh," she said.

"Apart from vague, and that won't do. What about, 'Sam Haigh, International Builder Extraordinaire'," I ventured.

"I don't think so. You didn't have anything on your van back home."

"Yes, I did. I had Sam Haigh, Todmorden, and my number, in flaky letters on one of the back doors."

"So you did. I guess you didn't need to advertise."

"No, and here... well, if I carry on with Darren and I spend a good few Saturdays at old Barry's, I guess I can't take anything else on for a while."

"Hmm, but you'll want to make the transition to working around here at some point."

"I guess so," I said, thinking how convenient it was to work for Darren, despite the long drive, rather than risking leaving him to take the plunge around Ontinyent, with all the logistics and uncertainty that it would imply. I might get a big local job, part company with Barry, finish the job, have nothing else lined up, and then find that he'd got someone else to work for him. Then I remembered that I'd no longer be earning such good money, as three or four hundred euros a month, if not more, would have to be set aside for my national insurance and taxes.

"A penny for your thoughts, love?"

"Oh, just weighing things up," I said, before filling her in on my conjectures.

"Just take things as they come," she said, not for the first time.

"Things were simpler back home, weren't they? We both enjoyed our work and didn't even talk about it that much, unless something interesting came up. Now it seems like we don't talk about anything else. I thought it'd be more chilled out living here."

"It will be, eventually," she said without much conviction, because apart from the atrocious traffic jams, something I'd tried to work around and which hadn't affected Emma much, we'd been pretty chilled out back in Todmorden, especially in winter.

I took a long swig of beer. "Why have we come here, Emma?"

"Why? Well, to have a better life, to enjoy the weather."

"There's no doubt about the weather being better, though it'll be tough at work in summer, but what else is there?"

"You're not having doubts, are you?" she asked, looking a little concerned.

"Not at all. I'm just speaking in general terms, you know, not just about us."

"Well, the weather's certainly the number one factor for most people who come, though I suppose most of them are bigger sun worshippers than us." Her brow creased in thought. "Given that our family unit's the same wherever we are, I suppose it'll depend on the friendships we make."

"Whereas being away from our families is a downside, on the whole," I said, as although my parents had spent a little more time at our house than I'd have liked, not seeing them at all seemed like too extreme a change. Ditto for Emma, I knew, with her folks, not to mention childcare, again.

Yes, but as you know, your dear in-laws will be with us less than a fortnight from now," she said.

"So soon?"

"I told you last night."

"Oh, yes, I was a bit sleepy. For a week, isn't it?"

"Eight days, including a full weekend, so you won't miss out," she said, before pinching my cheek.

"I'll give Barry a miss that weekend then, though I guess I could take your dad along. Him and Barry'd get on."

"We'll see. I won't be missing any classes. I want them to see that we're not living the life of Riley."

# 9

"Ooh, it's like being on holiday all the time living here," said Cathy, Emma's trim, lovable, caring, empathic and very talkative mother, who had arrived with father Dan in their hire car that very morning. It was a sunny Friday in late October and I'd knocked off at lunchtime, as Darren and I had just finished a job and had no desire to start the next one.

"It is *not* like being on holiday, Mother," said Emma who, like many daughters, only addressed her formally when she had a point to make.

By the time the sun had disappeared behind the pine trees, we'd brought them up to date on all our trials and tribulations.

"The main thing is that Luke's doing well," Cathy said as she cradled her long-lost grandson, who looked like he'd had enough pampering for the time being.

"Yes, it *is* the main thing, Moth… Mum, but there's us to consider too. It isn't easy, you know, starting a new life somewhere."

"No-one forced you to come here," said Dan with mock gruffness. "I think *I* could handle it very well," he added, before taking yet another sip of beer.

"It's easier for retired people," Emma said. Dan had been a canal worker and Cathy a dentist's receptionist, by the way, and they were both enjoying their fairly fit sixties, apart from Dan's haemorrhoids, a subject which I kind of hoped he wouldn't bring up.

"It's earning a living that's the tricky bit. You two, on the other hand, would have a whale of a time," I said.

"Yes, have you ever thought about moving here too?" Emma asked them, causing me to regret my rash words, as having Cathy in the next casita would be a very mixed blessing.

"Us? Well, I don't think we have, have we, Dan?"

"Nope. We've got too much to do back home," he said sharply, as if the idea had been proposed and rejected at some point. Though retired, Dan still volunteered as a lock-keeper and generally liked to hang around 'the cut', and as his suggestion of buying a narrowboat and chugging off around the canal network had been quashed by his wife, I guessed there was a bit of a stalemate regarding potentially revitalising projects. Besides, Cathy had a busy social life too, being involved in charity work and sundry other things, so – as I mentioned to Emma later – it would be stupid to give up their active lives just to be near their daughter and grandson.

"Ay, some of us still like England, you know," Dan said as we made our way into the rather chilly house.

"So do we, Dad, but we like this better, we think," said Emma.

"I hope so, love, I really do," he said, smiling at the blank TV screen, as he'd already been told there was no English TV, so he'd be spared all the soaps for a week.

Dan was more than happy to come with me to Barry's the next day and the two of them chatted amiably while I got on with knocking off the crumbling cement around the worrying crack, which didn't prove to be as house-threatening as I'd feared, though

I doubt it would have stood even a moderate earthquake. While we were eating the stew that Barry had made for our lunch, Dan asked him if he'd ever thought about going back to England.

"No, I shan't be moving from here now. There's nowt for me there anyway. Why exchange this…" he pointed out the olive groves and the mountains beyond, "for a terraced house or a crummy flat back in Derby?"

"Ay, it's grand here," said Dan, which was true if you kept your eyes averted from the house, though I was about to improve that part of the vista little by little.

"I've been here for the best part of fifteen years now, so there's no going back," he said, failing to call Dan duck as I'd hoped, so perhaps Derbyshire folk reserve that epithet for younger people.

It turned out that Barry was seventy-six, and he claimed that all the olive oil he'd consumed, the pies that he hadn't, and drinking red wine instead of beer had kept him feeling pretty nimble for his age, apart from the cancer, which he was still recovering from.

"It'll not come back, God willing," said Dan, an avowed atheist and, it appeared, a medical diagnostician, though he had put away a few glasses of Barry's healthy, heady red wine by then. "The cross I have to bear is my piles," he went on, so I went back to work.

"What did you think of Barry?" I asked him as we drove home.

"A grand bloke. Shame he's stuck here though."

"Stuck here? Do you think so?"

"Course he is. He's burnt his boats and there's nothing for him back home anymore. Mind you, there's worse places to end your days."

"Maybe when he retired he didn't have much to do at home, so he decided to come here. He worked at the Rolls-Royce factory, making aircraft parts. A huge place, he said."

"Ay, there's jobs that when you're done you're done. I've got the canal in my blood now and I can't stay away from it. You know, I think them that comes here to retire, they come because they've nowt to do at home."

"You might have a point there, Dan."

"Ay, I just wish Cathy'd come round to the idea of us getting a little narrowboat."

"Get one anyway."

"It's crossed my mind, lad. Get one while I'm still fairly fit," he said, nodding thoughtfully. "Though the damp's not good for my you know what."

The rest of their visit was pleasant enough, though after driving them up to the picturesque town of Bocairent on Sunday – where we strolled up to the cliffside caves, before exploring the narrow, medieval streets – I only saw them for a few hours each evening. They enjoyed spending time with Luke, as he did with them, and on the Thursday morning Emma did her first class with Caroline, Theresa and Jane, in Caroline's casita, which from her description I guessed must be near to the one that Brian, the chap I'd met in the bar, couldn't and didn't want to sell.

"Jane," I thought aloud.

"What about her?"

"The name rings a bell. Oh! Is her husband a bloke called Brian?"

"Er, I think so, yes."

"Did she say anything about eight verbs, about only needing eight verbs? Do you not remember the bloke I told you about a few weeks ago?" I asked, getting quite excited about this far from incredible coincidence.

"No, she was very quiet. It took me a while to get anything out of her, but come to think of it she did know quite a bit when she started feeling confident enough to speak."

I reminded her of Brian's eight-verbs-plus-a-few-words theory about getting by in Spanish.

"Well I'll be trying to teach her how to use them, though I'll have to go easy on the grammar or I'll scare them off. They're all really nice ladies and it's fun to teach them," she said, her eyes showing far more enthusiasm than after any of her English classes, which I mentioned to her. "Yes, it's more of a challenge and just… well, different. Teaching English to kids is as dull for me as it is for them, but my ladies enjoy it, and so do I. I'm so glad that I decided to put up the ads now."

And so was I, because while I was finding working for Darren pretty satisfying, as by then he'd begun to consult me about how to go about each job, I knew it had been a downer for Emma to go from teaching a classful of kids to poring through textbooks with feckless teenagers, though her classes with the two younger children were somewhat more rewarding. We both hoped that more Spanish classes would come up and maybe also a little interpreting work, though Helen, who we didn't see socially, seemed to have that side of things pretty sewn up.

Before Cathy and Dan left we said that we'd see them at Christmas, as I knew that Darren intended to go back for about ten days. A week and a half later my parents came out for a week, so we practically replicated the programme of events that seemed to have pleased Emma's folks. I took my dad with me to Barry's, where they chatted while I put in a new living room window, we visited Bocairent, and they made the most of their time with Luke.

I took their final day, a Friday, off work, and as we drove to Alicante airport a few pertinent things were said.

"Well, it'll soon be Christmas," my mum said, already a bit sad about being parted from her only grandson.

"So, do you think you've made the right decision?" my dad asked Emma over his shoulder.

"I think so, Bob. What do you think?"

"Well, you seem to be getting on all right, though I suppose young Sam here'll want to be working for himself before long."

My dad, who was physically an older version of me, plus a little potbelly that had developed since his retirement from his job as a bus driver, had been very proud when my building work had begun to prosper, partly thanks to him, as he had subtly networked in the pubs and clubs, extolling my skills and inherited honesty to his cronies. When I'd told him that I was working mainly for Darren, I think he thought I'd come down in the world a little.

"It'll take time, Dad," I'd said on the drive back from Barry's.

"Ay, I know, but I sometimes wonder why you chucked in that great little business you had."

"I know, but life's not all about work, is it?"

"I guess not, though I miss my job in a way," he said, as although he kept himself fairly busy, he didn't have any serious hobbies. "Oh well, maybe you'll come back some day. You'd soon find work, I'd see to that," he said, but I'll get back to our conversation on the drive to the airport.

"As more jobs come up, I'll work less for Darren and more for myself," I said.

"Hmm, for the Spanish or the British?"

"Probably for the Brits and other foreigners. There are plenty of good Spanish builders around."

"Hmm, so I guess you'll always be an outsider, and if Emma prefers teaching Spanish to other English folk, like she says, then… well, that won't help either," he said to me, causing me to grip the wheel hard, as this damning verdict regarding our integration prospects had come out of the blue.

"We've got two really good Spanish friends already," said Emma in the nick of time, as I'd been about to tell him that he wasn't being very helpful.

"Who? Those neighbours?" he asked with a frown.

"No, a couple, Álvaro and Chelo. We see a lot of them," she said, which wasn't strictly true, as although I saw Álvaro at least once a week, neither of us saw much of Chelo, as they often went off ballroom dancing – or Latin dancing, if that's the same thing – on Saturday nights, which Luke prevented us from partaking in, thank goodness.

"Well, *I* think it's wonderful here," said my mum, putting her own feelings aside to back me up, I deduced. "You're just jealous, Bob," she added, digging her finger into his shoulder.

"Ay, maybe so, maybe so, but time'll tell."

Did this curious conversation, I ask myself rather than my patient readers, have any effect on our future decisions? Quite the contrary, I believe, because when someone questions such a life-changing move as the one we'd made, your reaction is normally to stick to your guns and try to prove them wrong. To be fair to my dad, it wasn't a subject that he pursued on subsequent visits, but I think my mum might have read him the riot act before each of our get-togethers, though she would have danced for joy had we thrown in the towel and slunk back to Yorkshire.

When November arrived, with it came a distinct chill in the air, plus a few consecutive drizzly days which we hadn't experienced before, though we'd had a couple of tremendous downpours early in October. If we'd had central heating we'd have flicked it on for an hour or so now and then, but we were sure that the two gas heaters and the wood-burning stove would be more than enough to see us through the winter in comfort, and that we'd soon get used to the annoying pong of the bottled butane gas.

One Saturday evening I brought in some firewood from the last tenants' pile and lit the stove, partly to see how effective it was. The living room was soon as warm as toast and I felt sure that the stove would be more than sufficient for what a Spanish winter could throw at us.

"Will we have to buy another load of wood?" Emma asked me after lecturing Luke on the grave injuries he'd sustain if he touched the thing, as he'd thought the flames so lovely that he wanted to pat the glass.

"Nah, I doubt it. There's a good bit left," I said, referring to the square metre or so of wood that went up in smoke long before the end of the year, and I'll speed us along to that point in time as nothing much changed during November and December. I soldiered on with Darren and whenever I thought my Saturday job with Barry was coming to an end, he always thought of something else for me to do. I was sure by then that he was pretty well-off, because as well as his state pension he also received a handsome one from Rolls-Royce, and the work that occurred to him was all necessary – like changing more windows and doors, replastering and painting the walls, among other things – so I was more than happy to go on with my uncomplicated tasks and enjoy his pleasant company. I even took the odd day off during the week, usually between jobs, but I knew that sooner or later I'd have to get back to the three callers who'd made rather vague enquiries about my services and start building up my own clientele.

Emma's biweekly classes with her three ladies were going great and in December a Scottish couple got in touch, so she agreed to start teaching them at their tall, narrow house in the old part of town when we got back from our Christmas holiday, which would make a total of ten or eleven hours a week, with more students undoubtedly in the pipeline.

"Ha, that'll make us about €150 a week. I would've earned that in a day back home," she said one evening as she pored over her notes and textbooks.

"You also run the house and do my paperwork," I said, as although I'd helped out with the housework in England, I now had little time or energy to spare.

"I know, love, and I think I miss the kids and the school more than the money. That was a real career, whereas my classes here... well, I guess other things make up for it."

"Yes, I guess they do," I said, before chucking a couple more logs into the stove.

# 10

One of the most notable aspects of our nine days in Yorkshire were the trips there and back. After six months in southern Spain, the sight of all that greenery on the drive from Leeds-Bradford airport was a huge contrast to the more arid landscape around Ontinyent. I mean, there are plenty of pine trees and other foliage there, but this green seemed greener than any green we'd seen before. The traffic was denser than any we'd driven in before too, as in barely fifteen miles we saw more cars than we'd seen in six months, or so it seemed, as even the Ontinyent rush hours were nothing like this.

When Dan drove us onto the Bolton Brow estate in Sowerby Bridge, the houses looked closer together than they used to be, and I reflected that we really were privileged to inhabit our large casita with grounds that six of these semis would have fit into, gardens and all. It was a cold, drab day too, so apart from the greenery, our new home was coming out very much on top so far. We spent Christmas with Cathy and Dan, before they drove us down to Todmorden on Boxing Day. More greenery! More astonishing traffic! I thought, and though all this might sound daft, I'm sure that many people who live in warmer climes will have experienced similar sensations on their first trip back. Emma felt the same anyway, and she's at least as sane as me.

It felt good to be home, and as we were staying at my parents' house where I'd grown up, this feeling of nostalgia was especially acute. If you avoid the main roads, Todmorden is a pretty quiet place, and on the three crisp, sunny days we enjoyed before the New Year we headed up onto the moors and did some very pleasant walks, the last of them to Stoodley Pike, the memorial I mentioned earlier. This rather phallic stone structure was erected to celebrate the defeat of Napoleon, before falling down when the Crimean War was declared and being rebuilt in 1856, after we'd duffed up the Russians, despite the debacle of the Light Brigade. Fascinating stuff, I'm sure you'll agree, but what fascinated me that day was the fact that I'd compared it ironically to the peak of the Benicadell mountain on the day of our intrepid ascent.

"Do you know, Luke, that the mountain we climbed in Spain was almost three times as high than this?" I said to my son, his tanned face reddened by the cold wind.

"I like this better."

"Really? Why?"

"It's all green and I like the sheeps."

"Sheep," I said, glad that he was getting some intensive English practice, a lot of it through the TV speakers.

"I like it too, on a day like today," said Emma, who looked lovely in her posh down jacket that had remained with our stuff at my parents' house, but which she'd be taking back with her.

"I *like* it, obviously, but it can't compare to those vast vistas as far as the eye can see, can it?"

"Can't it?"

"No, and it'll be dark in two hours, and raining tomorrow."

"Ha, I know what you mean, Sam, but don't just dismiss this landscape. It takes a lot of rain to keep it green, but where will we be walking next summer?"

"Mucho calor," said Luke, meaning very hot.

"We'll go out at the crack of dawn," I muttered.

"Come on, we'll get back to the pub and you can have a pint of bitter."

"I think I prefer Spanish beer now," I said after we'd threaded our way through the people and dogs to the bar of the Shepherd's Rest Inn and managed to get served quite quickly. The real ale was delicious, but I still had a bee in my bonnet about my family's insistence on extolling the virtues of the land we had left behind. I guess that subconsciously I was so set on vindicating our move that I didn't like to hear Yorkshire praised too highly, while Emma, and especially Luke, were much more objective about the whole thing.

The next day it chucked it down from the late dawn to the ridiculously early dusk and I threw Emma a few smug glances as we whiled away the hours indoors. After one especially self-righteous gaze in her direction, she looked at the rain streaming down the window and said, "Remember, the Spanish summer's a bit like the English winter. We'll be stuck inside then too."

"Fiddlesticks," I said, for want of a better expletive. "At least we'll be able to soak up the rays for a bit, before having a lovely cold shower."

"Summer, piscina," said Luke, who I'd thought immersed in a CBeebies cartoon.

"Yes, and we'll be able to go to the swimming pool in town," said Emma, as Ontinyent has a great municipal pool that we'd discovered just before it closed for the winter, while the surrounding villages all have more modest ones.

"There you are then," I said with a grin. "And when we eventually buy a house it'll have a pool, and if it doesn't I'll build one."

"I wonder how many bridges will go over the water before then," said Emma.

"You're losing your English," my Mum said, looking up from her knitting.

"It's just a little in-joke we have, Mary."

"Ah, I wish I was there again." She scowled at the window. "I suppose we'll wait till it warms up a bit before we come out," she said, looking at Emma and me in turn.

"Easter would be good, as we won't be working," Emma said. "Though it's early next year, toward the end of March, I think."

"We'll see then. Bob and me want to get some decent sunshine, don't we, love?"

As my dad really had been immersed in the cartoon, it took him a while to answer. "Eh? Oh, yes, maybe we'll wait till May. Ha, 2008. When I was young the next century seemed like eons away. Let's hope it's a good year, especially for you three."

"I'm sure it will be, Dad," I said, little knowing that... well, what's coming won't be a surprise to those readers who keep up with the news, and I'm not talking about the Beijing Olympics.

I won't drone on about the great contrast I perceived when we arrived back in Spain, especially as the land around Alicante is as dry as a bone, but the sun was out, my car window down, and it almost seemed as if spring was in the air, silly as that may sound.

# 11

As by now I've filled you in on the state of play after our first half year in Spain, I won't bore you with every little detail of our day-to-day lives, and it wasn't until after Easter that we realised that something disturbing was in the air. On the news they'd been talking about the economic 'slowdown' during the short but sharp winter which arrived in January, but the consequences of this euphemistic term were yet to make themselves felt.

By the Easter holidays Luke was just about fluent in Spanish and not far off in Valenciano, and he was as happy as a sandboy at school, his sandy hair still seeming exotic enough to make him a prime mover in the social hierarchy of his class; that and his great personality, of course. Though he still played with Oscar and Claudia, he'd also made some new friends and we often drove him to theirs, or them to ours, and in the process met their mostly amiable parents, though Álvaro and Chelo were still our only real Spanish friends.

Emma had a total of sixteen hours' teaching by then – six in English and ten in Spanish – so she'd met more expats than me, though Caroline, Jane and Theresa were still her favourites by far. She thought that was enough work to be going on with, and I agreed, because what with one thing and another she was almost as busy as me.

In the New Year I'd gritted my teeth and telephoned the three potential customers who'd called me in December. Of these, only one of them, a well-spoken lady called Sophie, got down to brass tacks and asked me to give her a quote for a small extension to her casita. Of the other two, both British men, one had found someone else to pave his patio – causing me to kick myself for my tardy response – and the other said he was hanging fire for the time being.

"Why's that, if you don't mind me asking?" I'd asked him on the phone.

"Well, I don't like the look of the news. There are hints that the economy's starting to backslide a bit."

"So does that mean you no longer want a pool?" I asked, as although building a pool from scratch would test my organisational skills – contracting diggers, concrete trucks and suchlike – it would enable me to begin to break away from Darren and start to become my own man, though I'd have divided my time between his work and the pool, as Barry's house was just about finished by then.

"I still want it, but I'm worried about investing money in the house if prices might start to fall."

"Right," I said, wondering what the hell that had to do with his desire to bathe. I mean, surely these mature people didn't still think they were on the housing ladder, did they? After expressing my opinion that the news reports were unfoundedly pessimistic – as if *I* knew – I asked him to call me back if he decided to reconsider.

"We'll see, we'll see. Me and the wife are pushing seventy now and we can't be taking risks."

All the more reason to take risks, I thought but didn't say. "I expect you're right," I did say, before ringing off.

So, one Sunday morning in mid-January I drove up to Sophie's casita on the other side of town and was greeted by several overfriendly dogs. After calling them off, the lady of about sixty with short grey hair, billowing hippie-style clothes, and a friendly face led me around the small house to the site of her proposed extension.

"I've got eight now, you see, so they're becoming rather a handful in the house," she said with a refined titter.

"I bet they are. How come you've got so many?"

"Well, I took in a couple of strays, word got round, and more arrived, one of which I found tethered to my gate one morning. I've drawn the line for now, I think, but I need that kennel building badly."

"A kennel, right."

So this was the extension she'd mentioned, I pondered as I surveyed the proposed site, then a much trodden former vegetable patch. "Well, I guess I'd lay a bit of reinforced concrete and build on that, using breeze blocks, which I'd render and paint, and a corrugated roof," I said, foreseeing about a week's work if I didn't hurry.

"Oh, but they must be able to get into it from inside the house."

"What? I mean sorry?"

"Yes, I can't expect them to leave the others and walk right round the house at night. It would be like being sent to Coventry."

"Quite," I said, a word I rarely use in that context, so her posh accent must have rubbed off on me. "So…er, the roof?"

"Oh, like the rest of the house, I think. Don't you?"

"Absolutely. So what you really want is a proper extension, with proper foundations?"

"Yes, I suppose I do. How much will it cost?"

"Well, for a job of that size I'll have to do some calculations. I could take some measurements now and get back to you soon."

"All right, but could you give me a rough idea now?"

The house was decent, but nothing special, and her car was a well-used Nissan Micra, so I estimated her wealth and income to be middling to low, and she must spend a fortune on dog food. Some builders do these mental wealth assessments in order to decide how much to screw out of their more naïve customers, but that was not my intention, I assure you; rather the contrary in fact.

"Look, Sophie, I can build you a dog kennel like I described for about a thousand euros, but a proper extension will cost several thousand, maybe as much as ten, depending on how you want it finishing," I said, still feeling a bit confused by this kennel/extension quandary. I mean, would the dogs need double-glazed windows and a tiled floor, or would they be prepared to rough it? They were all mongrels, after all, so surely they wouldn't be too fussy. At this point, however, the agreeable lady helped me out.

"Let's not use the word kennel anymore then, Sam. I want an extension, fit for human habitation, which will just happen to house a few dogs for the foreseeable future."

"Righto."

"Let's measure where I want it, then you can toddle off and do your sums, but I think ten thousand is about tops for me."

"What about a conservatory?" I asked, stupidly, as specialist companies usually install those.

"No, no, it must keep them cool."

"Right, I'll just get my tape measure."

Aware of her maximum price, but wishing to build along the full width of the house, I therefore suggested a five by two-and-a-half metre edifice with a sloping roof slightly lower than that of the rest of the house, with three windows, a tiled floor, a security door, and a normal door leading into the house.

"That sounds splendid, Sam."

"Oh, there's one thing I ought to mention. I'll only be able to work on it for three days a week, as I have another job on down near the coast."

"My, you do get about. I'm in no great hurry, so I suppose that will be all right."

"I have to do an estimate for a dog extension," I told Emma on my arrival home at one, having sipped a couple of cups of Earl Grey in Sophie's hairy living room.

"A what extension?"

"An extension. I'll leave out the dog bit or I'll get confused again," I said, before relating the morning's events.

"Your first big job! Are you excited about it?"

"Yes, and worried, above all worried," I said, because as well as breaking the news to Darren that I'd only be able to do three-day weeks, I'd have to finally get to grips with the building scene in Ontinyent, having so far been mollycoddled by Arnaud and Barry; not to mention my estimate, which I already felt to be on the low side, having applied the £1000 per square metre rule of thumb on the drive home and realised that I'd cut things a bit fine.

"You big worrier!" she said, giving me a hug. "I'll help you to sort out supplies and things," she added, as she had a good idea of the logistics involved in building projects of this kind.

The next morning Darren nodded when I told him the news of the dog extension, but smiled broadly when I added that I'd still be able to work for him three days a week.

"Brilliant, I thought I'd lost you then for a minute."

"No, I know where my bread's buttered, and I like coming down here," I said, as it wouldn't have been manly to say that I enjoyed working with him, though I'm sure Álvaro would have said it, and probably grabbed his thigh too. I agreed to work the days that best suited him, but he also suggested that on rainy days we'd work on his latest apartment job, as he always contrived to have two things on the go, suggesting that the economic rumblings were yet to affect his trade. I asked him about this.

"So far so good, Sam," he said, tapping the handle of a nearby shovel. "I've seen the Spanish news too, and I guess things are bound to slow down a bit, but I got by OK during the last recession. It's the crap builders who'll struggle, not the likes of us."

"I hope you're right," I said, before we began to prepare the steel reinforcing bars for the foundations of the first swimming pool I was going to work on from beginning to end. I planned to make many mental and a few written notes, as if the non-risk-taking chap had thrown caution to the wind and asked me to build his pool, I'd have found myself on a steep learning curve, as people had started to say at about that time.

That evening I called Sophie and she seemed quite happy when I regretted to say that I couldn't do the extension for a cent under €10,000, so I guessed her other estimates had been higher, no doubt given by builders who were out to make a profit. Still, even if I made less than I'd have liked, I'd be getting my first proper Spanish job under my belt and Sophie was pleasant to be around, though I'd have to insist that her eight mutts be banned from the site. At that point in time our finances were pretty healthy, thanks mainly to my weeks of illicit earnings which I didn't feel guilty about as I intended to make a handsome contribution to the Spanish exchequer for many years to come.

I worked for Darren for the rest of the week, during which Emma made arrangements for the digger driver who Álvaro had recommended to go to Sophie's casita on Saturday morning, and the concrete company which Álvaro had recommended to pour their stuff in on Monday morning, which meant that I'd have to place the steel reinforcement bars that Sophie had ordered from the builders' merchant who Álvaro had recommended, on Saturday afternoon.

That terribly clumsy sentence is designed to illustrate the support I received from my friend and my wife, as Álvaro had the knowhow and Emma had just enough spare time to prevent me having to make a fool of myself on the phone, as I still found lip-reading and gestures to be a great aid to communication. At that time I felt that my Spanish had plateaued a little, as a weekly meeting with Álvaro and a few hours of semi-comatose TV viewing wasn't enough to keep improving. Emma seemed practically fluent to me by then, though she said she still had a way to go.

As I fear I might get embroiled in building and linguistic talk again, I'll move things on a bit. By Easter I'd finished Sophie's extension, to my, her, and her *nine* dogs' satisfaction, and in the meantime I'd landed a job which I relished. A Spanish, yes *Spanish* chap had asked me to quote him a price for a huge garden wall to be made of breezeblocks and clad with lovely stone that had, Álvaro said, fallen off the back of a lorry and into the compound of his impressive chalet in the vicinity of Albaida. Yes, it was through Álvaro that I got the job that ought to take me right through to August, when I planned to take the whole month off and spend most of it in cool, green Todmorden.

"It's a great, straightforward job that I'm going to enjoy, especially when I start with the stone," I told Emma when I'd sealed the deal.

"That's brilliant. Let's hope that while you're doing it something else comes up."

"Whoa, love! Let me celebrate getting this one first," I said, bottle of cava in hand.

"Of course, but I just saw on the news that the government's cut the growth forecast for this year."

"Yes, Darren says that things seem to be slowing down a bit down on the coast, but I don't think it's anything to worry about."

"No, but we'll keep our eyes and ears open and try to line you something up for after the summer."

Emma was still doing sixteen or seventeen hours' teaching a week and had also accompanied a couple of people to the health centre in order to translate their ailments to the doctors, as although most of them spoke some English, in medical matters misunderstandings might be fatal. Her English classes would start to tail off from the end of May, and we were both glad that she wouldn't have to traipse down to town four evenings a week and on Saturday mornings.

"I might kick them into touch this summer and try to get more daytime work," she said after sipping her cava.

"That'll mean Spanish classes, I guess."

"Probably, and hopefully more interpreting jobs."

"Not great for our integration then."

"No, but though I get on fine with my students' mothers, they never suggest us doing anything socially together."

"We've hardly got the time."

"No, but the odd Sunday lunch would be good. I mean, I love seeing Álvaro and Chelo, but it'd be nice to get another perspective too."

"Yes, it's not easy to worm our way into social circles here," I said, secretly quite glad that we couldn't, as I enjoyed our quiet Sundays together. Before coming to Spain I hadn't anticipated doing many six-day weeks, as I'd done few of them back home, but I knew that if I wanted to get established I'd have to tough it out for a year or two, I thought at the time.

One Friday afternoon towards the end of May I knocked off early down near the coast and called in to see Barry on my way home. I passed within ten minutes of his house every day that I worked for Darren, but hurry and fatigue had made me put off the visit for far too long.

"Hello, stranger," he said after propping his hoe against a plum tree. He'd put on a bit of weight and looked the picture of health, having finally overcome the ravages of his illness. His house looked healthy too, and there was no sign of the jagged crack through my cement, which he'd painted white by this time.

I patted Figo and sat down in the shade of the porch. "How's things, Barry?"

"Oh, pottering on, duck. I've been on a couple of trips with the Imserso, one to Peñiscola and one to the thermal baths in Fortuna."

"What's Imserso?"

"It's the Instituto de Mayores y Servicios Sociales," he pronounced slowly and clearly with barely a hint of his Derbyshire accent. "They organise tons of cheap trips and holidays for us old 'uns. It's a cracking way to meet folk. How are you doing, Sam?"

"Fine," I said, before filling him in on the events of the last few months.

"That's grand. It sounds like you're getting a foothold now."

"Yes, but I want to get another job lined up for after the summer," I said, hoping he'd think me premature.

"You do that. A little bird tells me there's going to be a bit less building work around soon, so you want to plan ahead."

"Which little bird was that, Barry?"

"Oh, a Spanish brickie who I sometimes see in the bar down in Castellón de Rugat. He works for a big firm on the coast and says that they've laid a few people off."

"Really?"

"Yes, only a few, mind, but it's been a long time since that happened, so he's a bit worried. For a while he was working six or seven days a week and bloody raking it in, but he's back on five now. Glass of wine?"

"Please, just a small one."

"Mind you," he said when he returned to the porch with the glasses, "I don't suppose those big new builds have much to do with what you do. If there *is* a recession coming, I think it'll take a long while for the kind of people you work for to feel it, if they feel it at all."

"Do you think so?" I asked, still a bit stunned by the news of redundancies.

"Oh, ay. They'll still want their pools, walls, extensions and whatnot, *but...*" he raised his finger a bit like Álvaro, "if folk lose their jobs you might find yourself with more competition. That's why you have to plan ahead, lad, and if the work does keep coming, you might be best to leave Darren and go it alone."

"Do you think so?"

"Well, that's up to you, but if things slacken off for him, it'll be you who suffers first."

"True," I said, grateful for this unwelcome news, if that makes sense. Barry had clearly given the matter a good deal of thought and I resolved to call in on him at least once a month from then on. Darren was still fairly upbeat about our prospects, but I think he was a born optimist, whereas Barry's more sceptical point of view was a sobering one that ought to keep me from getting too complacent.

The main reason I've described our conversation, apart from wanting to show that I'm not a man who completely forgets his friends, is to point out that in the late spring of 2008 I was probably more aware than most of the impending downturn, and as forewarned is forearmed, Emma, Álvaro and me, probably in that order, did our level best to find at least one big job for after the garden wall was erected.

# 12

The wall job, as I called it, was for a businessman who Álvaro bantered with in one of the innumerable bars where he dropped in for coffee to rest his weary legs while walking the beat. Most people treated Eduardo with some respect, because as well as dressing elegantly and driving a huge Mercedes, it was thought that some of his dealings were somewhat shady. As you probably know, nepotism and corruption are rife in Spain, but as long as a dodgy dealer or bent politician's shenanigans don't affect them directly, people tend to grudgingly admire them rather than despise and berate them.

So, Álvaro told me, while other folk all but doffed their caps to the stout man in his late forties, he never lost an opportunity to tease him regarding his rapid acquisition of wealth. I can't quote their conversations, of course, as I wasn't present, but I imagined that Álvaro's jocular greeting of Jose Manuel when I bought the van – calling him a thief, before shaking his hand – was probably the way he also treated the rather grim-faced entrepreneur.

When the three of us met, however, Álvaro was on his best behaviour, as I had a lot riding on that trip to the recently built chalet a couple of miles east of Albaida. We were inspecting the piles of flat stone when Eduardo pulled up in his Mercedes and I saw straight away that he was what our neighbour Juan wanted to be; a suave, self-assured *somebody*, as opposed to the harassed salary-slave that he would probably always be.

"Che, bon día, Edu," said Álvaro, to which the po-faced man responded likewise in Valenciano, before Álvaro introduced me in Spanish.

"This Inglés is the best builder of walls in the region, Edu. His wall will put the finishing touches to your marvellous country residence," he said with just a hint of mock subservience.

"I'm not going to live here," he said flatly.

"No?" I asked.

"No, I built it more as an investment. Once the wall is finished and the gates put on, I will sell. I think it is time," he said with a knowing look.

I wanted to ask him why it was time, but thought I'd better concentrate on the task at hand, namely to land the job, so I produced my thirty metre tape measure and, with Álvaro's help, measured the length of the proposed wall. Had Eduardo intended to live there, I think he would have opted for sidewalls too, as the land rose up from the track to the house, behind which lay a field of almond trees, but he told me that he would fence off the rest of the compound.

"The wall is merely to add value to the property. I have the stone, so I may as well use it."

I then convinced him that we ought to curve the twenty-eight metre wall round a bit at the ends, to make it look more stylish and add support.

"Yes," Álvaro chipped in. "A straight wall built by Sam may collapse after two hundred years, but with perpendicular support it will last for a thousand."

"I don't care how long it lasts after the house is sold, but I agree that it will look better," he said, scowling and scratching his pasty cheek, as he wasn't the type to get out in the sun much, unlike me.

After a few more measurements and notes, I told him that I'd call him with my quote.

"I have a price in mind."

"Oh?"

"Yes, I wish to spend six thousand euros."

"Right, well…"

"Can you build it for that?"

"Yes, but it depends how you want to finish it. There are details to discuss."

"Six thousand, in cash. Let me know what materials you need and they will be delivered."

This was sounding better all the time, but I didn't know quite what to say.

"Sam will do it," Álvaro said. "It's a shame that you are not to live in the house, as it will have the best wall for miles around."

"Shut up, Álvaro, you haven't a bloody clue about building," he said, or words to that effect. "Look at the hovel that you live in." He smiled for the first time, rather more brightly than I'd expected.

"I am a poor man… but honest," Álvaro said, grinning with pleasure, as the deal was all but done, so they could get back to their mutual joshing.

"How did he make his money?" I asked Álvaro on the drive back to town. Eduardo and I had shaken on the deal and I'd promised to make a start the following week and finish it before August.

"Well, his father was a notary, a clever man, and he has passed on a good deal of money and knowledge. Eduardo is not so clever, or not in the same way, and he left school early and began to deal in this and that. Then he bought a small textile firm, which he ran into the ground, before moving into property, among other things. I think it is the property boom that has made him rich."

"He said 'it is time' about selling the place. What do you think he meant by that?"

"Well, it seems that property prices are no longer rising, so maybe they will fall a little, who knows? I am glad I didn't buy a studio apartment on the coast as I was planning to."

"Good advice from Chelo, no?"

"Yes, I respect her opinion on such matters," he said, gazing at the mountainside.

The next two months were the hardest of my life, and both my parents and Emma's, during their almost consecutive visits in June, remarked that I was overdoing it a bit. I pointed out that I had to finish the wall before the end of July while still working for Darren three days a week, which was why I also worked on Sundays, unless I was simply too exhausted. It was the heat, of course, that really drained me, as although I was nearing forty I still felt as strong as an ox.

At the beginning of July, Álvaro found me a labourer, a rather boozy individual called Diego who hailed from Ecuador. Álvaro made friends with him one evening while in the process of arresting him for being drunk and disorderly, and suggested that I give him a few days' work and thus take the pressure off myself. It made sense to have a labourer for such a laborious job, but as I'd wanted to keep the whole six grand to myself, I'd been mixing and laying, mixing and laying, until I was fit to drop.

"He doesn't sound ideal, Álvaro."

"He has a heart of gold and is a good worker."

"Why is he not working then?"

"His work in the country has ended until September. You pay him ten euros an hour, plus a few litres of beer, and you will progress like lightening."

"I'll give him a try."

The faint smell of beer on Diego's breath as we drove towards Albaida didn't seem very auspicious, but when the lean, brown, black-haired man of thirty-three got cracking I saw that appearances could be deceptive. Though he drank almost as much warm beer as I drank water, he took the heat in his stride and I never found myself without material. As we ate our packed lunches on the two old chairs in the kitchen, Eduardo having kindly lent me the key to the house, I asked him what had brought him to Spain.

"Work, and work alone, Sam. We Ecuadorians love our country, but we earn much more in Spain, so we come."

"So don't you want to stay here?"

"No, our objective is almost always to make money, to pay for our houses or set up a little business back home." He munched his bocadillo and swigged his beer. "Though I am not very good at saving," he said with a wry smile.

The €860 that I ended up paying Diego for his work was money well-spent and I couldn't have finished the wall in time without him. Towards the end of the job, when I was building the gate pillars, Eduardo put in only his third appearance. After walking gingerly through the dust and frowning at my labourer, who looked very Indian with his headband and bare, well-defined torso, he expressed his satisfaction with my work. After explaining Diego's invaluable presence, I asked him if he wanted me to fit the gates.

"No, other men will do that. You have done enough, more than enough," he said, touching a gate pillar with his finger, before inspecting it for dust. He always wore a suit and tie, and I doubted he spent much time outside one air-conditioned environment or another. He'd paid me half the money by then and I was looking forward to getting the rest and saying goodbye to my open-air torture chamber, because though the views were good, I'd seen too much of them through the shimmering heat.

"Here's the rest of your money," he then said, handing me a thick envelope.

"Thanks, but I still have a little more to do."

"And I'm sure you will finish it. Would you be interested in more work?"

"Er, yes, but I'm on holiday next month."

"Naturally."

At that point in time, despite our efforts, I had no definite work lined up for September, apart from with Darren, of course. I had a few smallish things in the pipeline, but as inland Spain practically shuts down in August, I had as yet to shake a hand or sign on a dotted line.

"What do you have in mind, Eduardo?" I asked, as I'd never felt able to address him as Edu.

"I have several properties, some near here and some further away. I would like to begin to get them ready for sale, so there are many jobs to do, such as tiling and plastering and some minor building work. Painting too, but I have men to do that, of course," he said, sounding a bit proprietorial about his minions.

I'd have liked to have talked things over with Emma, but I didn't like to seem indecisive. "I could do any building work within one hour of Ontinyent," I said, trying to match his cool, confident gaze with one of my own, though a few drops of sweat soon put paid to that.

"Excellent. So, enjoy your holiday and call me when you get back."

"What about the keys for this place?"

"Oh, yes. Please give them to your policeman friend. He knows where to find me," he said, before patting me on the shoulder rather than shaking my filthy hand.

"Vale, but… well, are you sure there's a lot of work for me? I have other possible jobs, so I will have to tell them I'm not available," I said, losing my nerve a bit at the last minute.

"Many months' work, Sam. It is time to sell," he said, raising his eyebrows, before spinning on his dusty heels and marching back to his car.

"What about Jane and Brian's firewood shed, or whatever it is he wants?" Emma asked me when I told her the glad tidings.

"I felt that I had to make a decision there and then. He mentioned 'otros hombres' that he's got, and I wanted to snap up all the work I could. Besides, I don't want to work for that pillock Brian. I mean, all that haggling about a bit of a shed, and he'd be a pain in the neck to have around while I was building it," I said, as every time Emma saw Jane she collected more shed-related queries to pass on to me.

"Hmm, she *is* my friend, but I see what you mean. Well, if you think this tycoon of yours is trustworthy, go for it."

"I wouldn't call him trustworthy exactly, but he's paid on the nail, in cash, and you can't ask for more than that," I said, before handing over the wad of notes.

"I guess not. It's good that you're going to carry on with Darren though, so at least you've got your eggs in two baskets."

"Yes, I'm not doing so badly, am I?"

"No, but I'd like you to work a bit less after the holidays."

"Me too, but I'm glad Eduardo's got so much for me to do."

The truth was that I didn't even know where Eduardo lived, as his card only stated his name, mobile number and email address.

Álvaro knew that he had several properties in Ontinyent itself, and an undisclosed number elsewhere. He was married with two children, my friend said, but his car had often been spotted at the 'night club' between Adzaneta and El Palomar, not far from where I'd been building the wall. 'Night club' receives the apostrophes because in actual fact it was a brothel, which Spanish blokes don't seem to have much compunction about visiting, as you aren't obliged to 'go upstairs', so many claim to enjoy having a drink and chatting to the girls. I never visited that one or any other in all the time I was there, not because Emma is going to edit this manuscript, but because my English scruples prevented me from going to take a peek. I sort of wished I had done now, but there's time enough yet to satisfy my curiosity, as Spain isn't so very far away. Besides, old chaps form a considerable part of the clientele, I believe, so who knows if I won't sow my last wild oats in such a place? Emma will edit this out, but what the hell.

Back to Eduardo. Álvaro thought I'd done right to accept the work.

"Edu is a scoundrel, no doubt, but I think his dishonesty takes place on a higher financial plain," he said that Sunday at his casita, which I'd cycled up to, just to see if I could remember how to ride a bike. "In the town I have heard no rumours of him failing to pay anyone, so I think you have made the correct decision. Besides, when I gave him the key I warned him to treat you well, or I would chop off his balls and feed them to my pigs."

"You haven't got any pigs."

"Ha, he doesn't know that." He then scratched his nose, a sure sign that he was about to become serious. "No, joking apart, I have certain… knowledge about him which he knows I possess."

"What kind of knowledge?"

"Let's just say that it is a matter of skirts."

"But you already told me that loads of people have seen his car at that club."

"Pah, that is nothing. All men of his class frequent such places. If challenged by their wives they say they were entertaining a client, or some such nonsense. No, what I know is more... compromising. I have no intention of spoiling his fun, of course, just as I'm sure he has no intention of cheating you, so this is purely hypothetical."

"He definitely wants to sell his properties now. Do you think he knows something we don't?"

"Even small children now know that the housing boom is ending. I expect it will plateau for a while, and prices may drop a little, before things pick up again. It is cyclical, you see," he said sagely.

Despite Álvaro's hints about Eduardo's lurid lifestyle, I cycled home feeling happier about my commitment to working for him.

While I was slaving away in July I was pleased to know that at least Emma and Luke were taking it easy. As her English classes had ended she had plenty of spare time and they went to the large municipal pool in Ontinyent most days. One day they went to the much smaller but extremely pleasant pool in El Palomar, in order that I might join them for an hour or so at lunchtime, but the experiment wasn't a success. My refreshing swim made me feel so relaxed that I hated the idea of prising myself from the shaded sunbed, Diego away from the bar, and going back to work, so after that they only came a couple of times later in the afternoon, where I joined them after work, but only on days when Diego had been unable to come, as it was always difficult to get him away from the vicinity of a beer pump.

On the last day in July Darren and me gave each other a brief, manly hug and agreed to crack on with a vengeance in September.

He had two jobs lined up, more in the offing, and was cautiously optimistic about the future.

"Enjoy yourself in Taunton."

"You too in Todmorden," he said, having finally learnt to pronounce it correctly – Tod-mu-dun, more or less.

I dropped in on Barry on the way home.

"So you don't fancy going back home for a bit then?" I asked him over our glasses of wine.

"Not me, duck. I haven't been back for nine years, and I doubt I'll see that crummy island again."

"Oh, it's not so bad in summer," I said, as I was pining for my cool valley by then.

"I suppose not, but there's nowt for me there anymore. You makes your bed and you lies in it, eh?"

"There are worse beds."

"True."

# 13

We had a lovely, cool time in Todmorden and Sowerby Bridge, and Luke loved our four nights at the Center Parc near Penrith, though Emma and I preferred the next three, which we spent at a small hotel near Keswick. It rained for twelve of our twenty-six days in England – we know because we counted them – but despite that, it was great to be back in our green and pleasant land. We walked most days, even in the rain, and caught up with friends and other family members. It was a perfect holiday really, because while we enjoyed every single day, we were also looking forward to getting back; Luke to his school friends, Emma to her Spanish teaching which she wished to expand, and me to the promise of cooler weather and slightly less grafting.

"I shan't be working on Sundays anymore," I said one evening in the Hare and Hounds, where Emma and I had gone alone.

"No, I hope not, and you should really think about getting back down to five days. Life's cheaper there and at the moment we're rolling in money."

"True," I said, as the cheaper council tax, car insurance, energy bills and just about everything else certainly made a difference to our monthly budget. Eating out was cheaper too, though we'd been doing little enough of that. "I suppose we were rolling in money all the time when we were here, but we didn't think of it like that."

"No, and I guess we shouldn't now either. Then we were saving, and I suppose that's what we should be doing now too. We won't want to rent forever, however cheap it is."

"No. Anyway, I'll have to work at least three days a week for Eduardo, so I might see if I can cut my days with Darren down to two," I said, the holiday, plus the beer, having made me feel more relaxed and less grasping than I'd become. In England I'd paced myself because I'd always known that my next job was just around the corner, but wasn't that also the case now? "Yes, we'll be able to spend more time together from now on."

"I'm glad. We didn't move to Spain to work ourselves to death."

In the event, Darren was less dismayed than I'd expected when I told him that I wished to cut my days down to two. I'd met with Eduardo by then, and after we'd toured five of his properties in his purring Merc, I knew that I had enough work to last me for several months.

"I want you to begin on the house near Pou Clar," he said, referring to the clear natural pools to the south of the town. "Please finish the patio and put up the stone balustrades that my men will deliver."

"OK."

"I may, however, ask you to leave that job and go to the house near Aielo de Malferit to plaster those rooms we saw."

"Vale."

"Or the one in Agullent, to finish the garage."

"OK," I said, before giving my head a good scratch.

"It all depends on potential buyers, you see. I have put the houses you have seen up for sale, so depending on the interest that each property generates, one may take priority over another."

"I see, so they are all for sale, are they?"

"Yes, the time is right to sell now. The boom is over, I'm afraid, but I will make a good profit, I hope," he said, a shadow of doubt passing over his impassive face, I thought, though it might have been my imagination.

"Yes, I think I'll manage if you come on the days that I most need you," Darren said when I broke the news to him the following day, a look of relief passing over his slightly worried face. "One bloke gave me backword last week on quite a big job."

"Why was that?"

"I dunno. Seemed to have got the jitters about spending the cash. Another guy's umming and ahhing about a pool he wants too."

"Hmm, I know the news is a bit worrying, but I don't see why that should affect people having pools built or whatever. I mean, they've got the money, they want the pool, so what's the problem?"

"Well, you know what folk are like. Word gets round that prices might drop and they shit themselves. Not to worry, it might just be a blip, and I've got enough to be going on with."

"Yes, me too, I think." I'd told Darren all about Eduardo by then and he'd been pleased about my prospects even before the holidays, but especially now.

"Yes, I think you've struck lucky there, Sam. You never know, I might be asking *you* for work sometime soon," he said with a laugh.

"Do you think so?"

"No, just joking. I've built up quite a reputation among the expats along this bit of the coast. If I end up without enough work, God knows what'll happen to the others."

"Ha, ha, yes," I said, tapping the shaft of my hammer with my thumb.

"It's funny, just when I'd decided to concentrate on Spanish classes, there seems to be a big demand for English," Emma said on the Friday evening after I'd completed my first five day week for a long time. Though well rested after my holiday, I was still looking forward to a whole weekend with my wife and son.

"Have you had some calls?"

"Yes, one from a girl who's just finished an engineering degree, one from a mother – the usual sort, you know, worried about her kid failing at school – and one from that language school up near the new park."

"Right, what did you tell them?"

"First of all, that I'm only available between nine and three. That put paid to the mother's hopes, so I suggested she call the language school."

"Oh, and what did they say?"

"Well, they really wanted me in the evenings, but said that there might be something during the day. I asked about the pay and they said twelve euros an hour, so I said no way. They said they'd get back to me. Maybe I shouldn't have been so rash."

"Not at all, love. Stand your ground, especially if you're making fifteen or twenty elsewhere. What did the student say?"

"She's a graduate and she desperately needs to improve her English, as she wants to go and work abroad. She'll be coming here on Tuesday and Thursday mornings for two hours a time. I said sixty a week and she agreed straight off," she said, her face glowing with restrained pleasure. "So that'll be me just about booked up, unless I have students here in the evenings."

"No, no, don't do that. Let's keep the evenings to ourselves. Now that I'll be home by six some days we can start to have a proper family life again."

"Yes, I think it's going to be a good winter. Shall we watch that new Life on Mars DVD?"

"Yes, great," I said, glad of a rest from Spanish TV and adverts, as we no longer needed the listening practice. I still made loads of mistakes when I spoke Spanish, but I could understand just about everything by then, and quite a bit of Valenciano too. Emma sometimes read of an evening, but due to the tiring nature of my work I found goggling mindlessly at the box more relaxing.

Being more used to the heat by then, I enjoyed my work during September, and the fact that it was cooling down all the time was an added bonus. I finished the patio and balustrade at the house near Pou Clar without interruption, as Eduardo had only called round to pay me and silently admire my work.

"Am I going fast enough?"

"I think so, yes."

"Have you had many enquiries about the houses?" I was bold enough to ask.

"Some."

"Right, so you want me to do the Aielo house next, no?"

"Yes," he said, looking a bit distracted, before patting my shoulder and strolling back to his car.

"Where next?" I asked Darren when we'd fitted the last door on a house near Gandía. He didn't usually do doors, as he found them fiddly and preferred to call in a joiner, but he'd made an exception for his German customer.

"We've a big wall to build around a chalet near Denia."

"That's quite a way away, isn't it?"

"Yes, but it's a good job. It seems the owners are worried about burglaries all of a sudden. How are you getting on over your way?"

"Can't grumble. Still three more decent jobs to do after the one I'm on."

"And after that?"

"Well, I hadn't really thought about it."

"You'd better put some feelers out, plan ahead," he said, his brow more creased than I'd seen it before.

"Are you worried?"

"Well, yes. After the walls I've only got a couple of piddling things to do. Things have really taken a dive. It's not just property now, but the banks are shaky too. It's a real crisis of confidence."

"Listen, Darren, if you want to do the wall on your own, that's fine by me. It's a hell of a way for me to drive, so why don't you do it yourself? It'll make it last longer, till other things come up."

"Yes, that might be best. I wasn't going to suggest it, mind… but it might be best."

"No problem. We'll stay in touch and before long we'll be working together again."

You can see the way things were heading, but when I tell you that by December Darren was working with me on a house of Eduardo's not far from Barry's place, you'll know that matters had taken a serious turn. He still had the odd job to do, but as it wasn't far for him to drive I thought it was about time I gave him a helping hand, though after that I only had two more houses to finish off for Eduardo, who was yet to sell any of them. His Merc had been dustier of late, and I once spotted a tiny stain on his tie, so although his demeanour was as composed as ever, I suspected that all was not well with the roving capitalist.

"I suggest that you both slow *right* down," Barry said to Darren and me one afternoon as we sat sipping wine on his porch.

It had poured down after lunch, so we'd knocked off and driven over to see him.

"We're not rushing now," I said, gazing at his dripping allotment.

"No, but you've got to make the jobs you've got last till something else comes up," he said, more to Darren than to me, as he knew that I was still good for at least a couple of months. "Neither of you have mortgages, have you?"

"No," said Darren.

"Just the rent," I said.

"Hmm, why not just work three days a week for a bit? Tighten your belts and wait for other things to turn up. When folk ring you it's good to have the sound of a cement mixer in the background. It shows you're busy."

"But they don't ring, Barry," said Darren. "If anyone had told me a year ago that things'd be like this, I'd have said they were nuts." He shook his head before finishing his wine. "The wife's having kittens. She wanted to get all the family out for our silver wedding anniversary next March and I've told her to hang fire. We can get by, no problem, but there'll be no money for stuff like that."

"I've been thinking about getting this crummy patio relaid," Barry said, looking down at it.

"Liar," I said with a chuckle.

"No, honest, so whenever you want... you know, it is strange that it's gone so dead. I mean, if my income hasn't changed, nor will that of other retired folk."

"Some of them think the world's going to end," I said, thinking of Brian, who had told Emma that their house had started to lose value. He'd looked like he was about to cry, she said, which made her bite her lip so as not to laugh, as few people were sitting prettier than him and Jane, with their *four* pensions, as opposed to our none, something that had begun to worry us a little at that time.

"The world's going to end for all of us one day, some sooner than others, so you'll bloody well do my patio for me," said Barry, before filling our glasses.

"Thanks, Barry," Darren said, before knocking back his wine and pushing himself to his feet. "You know, I'm going to take your advice and work three days a week. Sod paying for hotels for a load of folk I haven't seen for donkey's years. Sheila and me can live on that and tough out the hard times ahead."

"Right, I'll see you on Monday then," I said to Darren, the wine having gone to my head a bit.

"But today's only Wednesday."

"Yes, so our three-day week is up," I laughed. "I'm going to do the same as you; make the work last and weather the storm," I said, keen to get home to tell Emma about my bold decision.

She agreed that, all things considered, a three-day week was the best plan. "We've had a good year, money-wise, and we can get by on a lot less. It'll give you a chance to get out on that bike of yours and enjoy yourself a bit for once."

"I enjoy working, usually."

"Yes, but you used to cycle too. The main thing is for you not to be idle. If you weren't such a philistine, you could read more, but as you don't you'll have to go cycling and see more of Álvaro."

"Our only Spanish friend, well, Chelo too."

"What about Eduardo?"

"Ha, he's hardly a friend, though we get on well enough. He still hasn't confirmed what I'll be doing next. He's due to pay me next week, so I expect he'll tell me then."

# 14

Our Christmas in Yorkshire was a little more sombre than our summer holiday had been, but we enjoyed it all the same. Eduardo had paid me the two thousand that he owed me and said that he'd call me in the New Year, so with my work for him, Barry's patio, and another small job that Emma had found for me, I reckoned I'd have enough to keep ticking over until the spring.

My parents and Emma's had different views regarding our lives and prospects in Spain, and in Sowerby Bridge we received Cathy and Dan's slightly more positive take on things. After I'd summarised events since the summer, Cathy took off her glasses and smiled.

"Things don't sound so bad to me, Sam. Like you said, you've been earning good money for a long time, so you can afford to take it easy for a bit. That's what Spain's all about, isn't it?"

"Not really, Cathy. Life goes on there just the same as here. Before, we were both earning good money all the time, and though it's true that a few quiet months won't matter much, at the end of the day we want to get on like most other folk."

"And we have to think about pensions too," said Emma, broaching a subject that we'd sort of skirted round until then.

"Yes, what's the score there?" Dan asked.

"We're in no-man's-land at the moment," said Emma. "We've got nowhere near enough paid in here, and there, well, I'm contributing nothing and Sam's paid in for just over a year."

I sipped my beer, for it was Christmas Eve, and prepared myself for a few home truths. Emma's no-man's-land statement made me conjure up flying bullets and water-logged shell craters, but it was the latter image which stuck in my mind. You don't get shot for not having good pension prospects at forty, but if you think about it rationally you certainly get a wallowing or even a sinking feeling.

"It's really a question of whether or not we plan to end our days there," said Emma, the reference to death doing nothing to cheer me up. "If so, I'll have to think about making contributions, and we ought to start private pension plans there too."

"Won't you end up in a sort of half-way house that way?" Dan asked, upon which I went for another can of strong bitter, intending to drown my sorrows.

"Well, we'll get *something* from here, and quite a bit from there, so I guess we'll manage," said Emma, before pointing at her glass, suggesting that she'd talked herself into a mood which she wished to lift herself out of, so I poured her some wine.

"Oh, stop worrying!" Cathy cried. "What a thing to be talking about at Christmas! Look, forget about it for a couple of years and then make a decision," she said.

"Yes," I said, liking what I'd heard.

"Two years from now you sit down and say, well, do we stay or do we go back," she said, which I liked a lot less. As far as I could see there was no getting round this no-man's-land business, but the two-year plan was about as good as it was going to get.

"Anyway," Cathy went on, all smiles, "if there's going to be a bit of a recession, you'll just have to take advantage of your free time and do all the things that *I* would do if I lived there." She inclined her head towards her husband by her side and tittered mischievously.

"What would *you* do, Mother?"

"Oh, sunbathe and swim, have drinks on that nice terrace of yours, go for little strolls in that lovely countryside, you know."

"It's seven degrees and drizzly there today," said Emma, who went online a lot more than me.

"Yes, well, of course, but winter'll soon be over."

I thought about the ton of firewood that we'd had delivered and which might just see us out. "No, it won't, Cathy, not for two months anyway, but you're right about us taking it easy. I've been working hard for over twenty years, we've got a house with good tenants in it that's practically paid for, and we've got plenty of money in the bank."

"And I've paid fifteen years of my teachers' pension, and you've paid about twelve into the one you took out, so things aren't so bad."

"Exactly," said Cathy, clapping her hands. "Let's drink to that."

"You've had enough," said Dan.

"Oh…. tosh! And I've a good mind to take you to live in Spain too." She grabbed his thigh a bit like Álvaro occasionally grabbed mine, only harder.

"Ow! Give over! Anyway, there's no canals in Spain, or none to speak of."

So, that being the upbeat opinion of my in-laws, you might be able to imagine my dad's view of my fading fortunes. As I said earlier, my mum had forbidden him from frowning upon our decision, but his weighty silences when the subject was mentioned were worth a thousand words. Luckily I'd been reading his Daily Mail, so I countered his slightly negative vibes with a few pertinent comments.

"Britain's going into recession too," I said one evening after Luke had gone to bed and we'd all gathered around the box.

He nodded and turned the sound down. "Yes, it's the likes of Spain that's dragged us into it."

"Oh, come on! It's a global thing. I mean, it's true that they went a bit mad building houses over there, but things aren't going to be great here either."

"No, not great, but, as you'll know if you read the papers (meaning the Daily Mail), there's still a housing shortage here, whereas in Spain there's about two million properties standing empty."

"Yes, well, but things'll slow down here too."

"Slow down, yes, but not die a long, agonising death like the Spanish economy. I expect we'll have to bail the buggers out before long, after we've sent ships over to pick up our ruined countrymen."

This was eloquence indeed for my dad, and if you remember that the Greek crisis didn't start until later that year, his talk of bail-outs was quite prophetic in a way.

"I'm confident that we'll weather the storm anyway."

"You'd have weathered it better here."

"Bob!"

"Sorry, love. Let's watch Morecambe and Wise."


I did say that we enjoyed our holidays, and apart from these conversations our economic prospects were hardly alluded to at all. One morning before the New Year I was strolling around the town, well wrapped up against the cold, blustery wind, when I saw three builders erecting some scaffolding. It didn't start raining until I got home, but they'd be out there, bolting the bars together, and I didn't envy them one bit. No, if necessary I'd attach a megaphone to my van and tout for trade far and wide, and if I ever got a bit down about things I'd remember those guys back home, out in the cold and rain with six hours still left to work, not to mention the rest of the winter.

No sooner had we got back and unpacked our bags than I received the year's first piece of bad news. Eduardo called to say that he didn't want me to start on either of his last two jobs for a while.

"How long is a while, Eduardo?"

"It's hard to say, Sam. My finances aren't as fluid as I would wish and I must sell a house before we can proceed," he said in his usual unperturbed tone.

"I see. Well, please call me as soon as you have anything for me."

"I will, and I'm sorry. Adiós."

"Hasta luego," I said, as adiós sounded a bit too final for my liking.

Emma received the news with a brave smile, before suggesting that I retile Barry's patio alone, rather than sharing the job with Darren.

"It's all about having *some* work now, as I'd hate to think of you hanging around the house all day, every day."

I looked at the film of drizzle on the window. "Yes, I guess so. That little job you mentioned before Christmas, who was it for?"

"Oh, for a chap called Robert who goes to the British bar. It's just a bathroom, I think. I've got his number on my mobile."

"I hate doing bathrooms. It's so enclosed and… fiddly," I said, as like Darren I preferred substantial, straightforward jobs in the great outdoors.

"Well, there's always Brian's firewood shed."

"Oh, God, not that. I'll ring that bloke then. I want to save Barry's patio for an emergency," I said, as I feared that my friend would think of something else for me to do after that, and I didn't want him to end up with a three-storey chalet and no money in the bank.

The bathroom bloke's voice rang a bell, and when I met him in the bar the following morning I found to my dismay that it was the one who had rudely cut short my attempts to converse on my first ever visit to the dratted place. I introduced myself to the big, flabby, red-faced man who looked a few years older than me, and received a twisted smile by way of reply.

"I'll show you what I want doing," he said in his whiny cockneyish voice, before slapping a coin on the bar and heading for the door. I'd fancied a quick coffee, but I asked the great lump if I should follow him in my van.

"Nah, let's both go in your van and you can drop me back here. I've fack all to do there and I'm sick of the sight of the place."

"Righto."

As we drove up towards the train station on the outskirts of town he told me that he wanted to replace the avocado bathroom because he was selling up and going back to England.

"Why's that?"

"'Cause it looks facking awful."

"No, I mean why are you going back?"

"Fack all work to do, that's why. I've been flogging property and that's dried up so I'm facked," he whined, and I transcribe his cussing in such a way because he really did pronounce it like that. His large chalet near the station was so nice that I was surprised that the second bathroom had stayed avocado for so long. I mentioned this.

"Never used it. Been up here on my own since the wife facked off, but I'd better get it done now. I want it in white, as cheap as possible."

I gave him a competitive quote and he nodded, before extracting his wallet and counting out the notes.

"You could have paid me afterwards," I said, venturing a polite laugh.

"No-one facks with me if they know what's good for them," he said with a particularly nasty look, more at the bath than at me.

I assumed his associates dealt with any miscreants, because though he was a big man, he was so flaccid that I'd have had no trouble fending him off. On the drive back down to the bar, where it appeared he spent most of his time, he became quite loquacious and told me why he'd decided to hop it. He was sure that property prices were about to fall sharply, so he was going sell his house at a reasonable price while he still could.

"I'll get two hundred for it, though I'd have got at least fifty more a few months ago. I can't afford to let it drop any more as I've got to buy something back in Kent. I thought I was facking rich when I sold up there ten years ago. I bought that place for a song and stashed half a million in the bank. Now I'll need most of it just to buy a facking semi."

"Right, that's tough," I said with all the sympathy I could muster. I didn't ask him what he planned to do in England, mainly because I didn't care, but I feared that his prospects weren't good, though with people like that you never can tell. Among his own folk he might have been considered a smooth talker, for all I knew of southern ways. As I wanted to sever my ties with him as soon as possible, I shelved my three-day plan and cracked on with the bathroom. When I returned the door key to the bar a week later I found him in great spirits, inside and out, as he'd found a buyer for the house.

"Who's buying it?"

"A facking Swede. A cunning looking cant who thinks he's got a bargain, but he'll see, oh, he'll see," he said, slurring his whiny words. "Have a shot, mate."

I accepted the shot of whisky and asked him what the Swede would see.

"I *know* the property game, mate, and prices are going to drop so far in this shithole of a country that you'll need a facking microscope to see them."

"That bad?" I asked hoarsely, having just knocked back my drink.

"If not worse. If I was you, I'd sell up and get out now."

"We're renting," I said, enjoying the feel of the word on my tingling tongue.

"Lucky you. What's your name, by the way?"

"Sam," I said, but I declined the offer of another shot, as despite his belated mateyness, I wanted to get away from his presence, not because he was so awful, though he was, but because I doubted that a continuation of our conversation would do much to cheer me up. OK, we were renting, but the rent still had to be paid.

"Don't worry about the rent, Sam. What I'm earning now just about covers our costs," Emma said after I'd reported back to her.

"What'll I do now?"

"You could do a bit of cycling, or build Brian's firewood shed."

I glanced at my dusty bike on the patio and before I knew it I was pumping up the tyres and oiling the chain. That afternoon I stashed my remaining flyers into my back pockets and toured all the suburban lanes around the town, leaving the sheets under windscreen wipers and impaling them on gates, as I'd forgotten to take my sticky tape. When I slogged back up the hill to the house, with wobbly legs and a sore bum, I decided to take a week off and dedicate myself to sport and publicity.

After getting five hundred flyers printed and buying several rolls of tape, I planned my daily routes and during the following week I *plastered* the villages and countryside with my advert. The weather was cold but dry and I found the task doubly satisfying, as besides feeling that I was doing my level best to secure whatever work was still around, I also found the cycling quite therapeutic and I'm sure that the endorphins my pedalling produced helped to stave off any feelings of despair.

The results of my campaign were two enquiries: a request for a quote for a small outhouse to house a pool pump and filter, and an offer of a fortnight's dog-sitting work, the payment being the use of the house and a fridge-full of food. I regretfully declined the latter, but I did build a stylish pump and filter kennel near a wealthy Norwegian's kidney-shaped pool, willing my mobile to ring as I toiled. It didn't ring, so a few days later I presented myself at Brian and Jane's house and sheepishly announced that I was finally free to build a home for his firewood.

"Hmm, you've certainly taken your time, young man," said my nemesis, as although his wife Jane was pleasant enough, my first and only meeting with Brian had made a lasting, unfavourable impression on me which his pompous smile did nothing to dispel.

After beckoning me over to the site of his proposed structure, he then went into great, incoherent detail about what it was that he wanted.

"So, you want a breezeblock shed with some metal racks to put the wood on?"

"Yes, but, as I say, I'm not sure if I want five racks or six," he said, screwing up his ugly face and scratching his head, upon which a few stray grey hairs were blowing in the cold breeze.

Decisions, decisions, I thought. "I'll get six and I can always take one back," I said, as they'd got to know me at the builders' merchant in San Rafael by then and they seemed increasingly glad of the trade.

I then quoted him a very reasonable price and he pulled a face. "That sounds a bit dear, Sam. Times are hard and the house is losing value as we speak. I only installed a wood-burning stove to cut down on the bills, so I mustn't exceed my budget."

"Well, our firewood is just leant against the house and the rain doesn't seem to do it any harm," I said, twirling my keys and taking a step towards my van.

"All right then. I know you need the work and I'm sure you'll pay attention to detail."

Over the coming week Brian didn't cease to pay attention to me paying attention to detail and the result of my labours was a mini-house with a roof to match his chalet's. He even insisted on a door, though I charged him extra for that, but when Emma totted up my costs it turned out that I'd been working for a pittance.

"Oh, never mind. They're ever so pleased and Jane's promised to praise you to the heavens, so something good might come of it."

"He took advantage of me, the bastard. I hope the value of his house drops to zero."

"Jane's planning a class lunch, but husbands are invited too," she said, raising her eyebrows in expectation of what was to come.

"No *way* am I feeding from the same trough as him, and if Caroline's bloke's a golfer and Theresa's is a DIY nut, I'd rather you made my excuses."

"Geoff's not doing much DIY now. They're thinking of going back to England, in fact."

"Really?"

"Yes, I think they feel a bit like that awful man you did the bathroom for. They're from Suffolk, you see, and they think that if they don't sell up now, they'll never be able to go back."

"I didn't know they wanted to go back."

"Well, they didn't, but they liked having the option. I guess no-one wants to feel trapped."

"They could move up north and buy a cheaper house. They'd welcome them with open arms in Yorkshire. He could buy a place in Tod and go down the pub with my dad and talk about DIY, ha ha."

"Sam, you're beginning to rave," she said with a chuckle. "Go and do some proper bike rides this week. Drop in on Barry and see what he has to say. He always seems to cheer you up."

"He'll want me to do the patio that he doesn't need. He's my last straw. After that I'll be a kept man."

"Oh, I don't mind keeping you for a bit," she said, before steering me into the bedroom, so at least I found out that my increasing stress levels hadn't yet made me impotent.

# 15

The next two months were memorable ones, but for all the wrong reasons. After paying Barry a social call on my bike via the spectacular mountain road from Beniarrés, I ended up doing his patio after all, but after that I had practically nothing to do. Darren was in the same boat, so he'd decided to build a small extension onto his chalet, which I'd visited once and met his very brown and rather scatty wife Sheila.

"Is that a wise thing to do, Darren, things being as they are?" I asked him on the phone.

"Oh, house prices don't bother me at all. We're planning to stay on regardless and it's something I've been wanting to do for a while. To tell you the truth I find it quite soothing to work on my own house, taking my time, and it stops me worrying about work."

"I go cycling to tire myself out," I said, as by that time – the end of February – I'd toured just about every road in a thirty mile radius of home. In Yorkshire February's not ideal for cycling, but there the cool air and often sunny skies were perfect for my long, steady rides. I normally stopped off at a bar somewhere for a bocadillo, always leaving a couple of flyers on the off chance, but a month later the only job I'd done was a roof repair for a friend of Álvaro's.

"We'd better think about taking you off autónomos if nothing comes up soon," Emma said one mild evening as we sat on the patio drinking tea.

"I guess so. We can't be paying two hundred-and-odd a month for nothing."

"Should we think about going back to England?"

"What? Things aren't so desperate, are they?"

"Not desperate, no, but I can't see things getting better any time soon. Quite the contrary, in fact, as the government's just announced that it's bailing out a savings bank, and unemployment is rising all the time."

I tried to avoid watching the news by then, but there was no doubt that Spain was in dire straits.

"I mention it because I'm just about in time to apply for jobs for next September. I doubt I'd get one near Todmorden, but I'm sure I'd find something in the north. That'd give us security and you could start looking for work."

"Building work won't exactly be abundant there either, and besides, Luke's so happy at school," I said.

"I know, that's the worst thing."

"The worst thing is going back and feeling like a failure," I said. Darren had told me that several would-be builders had already packed up the trowels they scarcely knew how to use and gone back home, but neither he nor I fitted into that category. "Oh, let's give it another year. Surely some folk'll still need things building and when all the riffraff clears off only the real builders will be left. I mean the foreign ones, as God knows what all the Spanish brickies'll do."

"They go and work in the country, by the sound of things. A lot of immigrants are leaving now, as the dole only lasts for so long here. OK then, I won't look for a job, but you'll have to keep your chin up, whatever happens. Luke worries when you look so gloomy. He can sense that things aren't going well."

"I will," I said, lifting my chin and stroking hers. "Let's just hope that a half-decent job comes up soon."

At the beginning of May Eduardo phoned me. In the meantime I'd painted the flat of an acquaintance of Emma's, built a dog-proof garden wall for Sophie, and cycled many miles. I'd also done many school runs and shopping trips, of course, as Emma's days were increasingly packed. She was getting more interpreting work by then, some of it for people who were going back to Britain. In one case they were leaving the keys of their unsold house with friends, while another family had accepted a very poor price and would be renting back home. In the following two years many people handed in their keys at the bank, leaving them to do as they saw fit with the still mortgaged properties, though it was Darren who was to tell me this, as it occurred more down on the coast.

I was glad to hear Eduardo's monotonous voice and I asked him how things were going.

"I have finally sold one of my properties. The house you worked on near Pou Clar."

"Great, did you get a good price for it?"

"No."

"Right, I'm sorry."

"But it is sold and I now have a little more liquidity. I have a proposition for you."

"A job?"

"In a way, yes. Can we meet?"

"Of course. In town?"

"Let's meet at the house near Albaida where you built the wall."

"When?"

"In one hour?"

"OK, I'll see you there," I said, happy with the idea because talking to Eduardo on the phone was like having a chat with the speaking clock.

When I arrived forty minutes later, Eduardo's Merc was already there. It was clean, but he was nowhere to be seen, so I pushed open the front door and called his name. He strolled out of the main bedroom, wiping his unsullied hands, and smiled. We shook hands and he patted me on the shoulder, bringing back fond memories of those bumper cash paydays of yore.

"So why have we met here, Eduardo?"

"Because I want you to live here."

"What?"

He chuckled and led me out onto the patio, where I noticed a table and chairs for the first time. This made me realise that there was quite a bit of furniture in the house too, and after another couple of seconds my razor-sharp brain perceived that it had come from the house that he'd sold.

"This is my proposition, Sam. You and your family (who he'd never met) come to live here. You pay me a very modest rent and in return I ask you to look after the place for the next two years."

"Two years?"

"Two years guaranteed, probably longer. This house is no longer for sale. It is too good to sell cheaply, and, well, my father gave me the land and it has a certain sentimental value," he said, showing no trace of sentiment. I didn't know if his father was alive or dead and didn't ask as I had other things on my mind.

"Well, thanks, but we're already renting a house in Ontinyent."

"I know. I know the owners. Such a shame they didn't build a pool," he said, glancing over at the pool, whose blue canvas cover was covered in about an inch of dust. "It isn't good to leave a house empty for too long. I may sell one of the others, if I have to, but this house will not return to the market until prices have risen again."

"How long do you think that will take?"

"Several years, but no matter. I intend to retire for a while as there will be absolutely no way for me to make money in Spain for a long time. I will try to enjoy my leisure time and the wealth I have acquired over the years."

"You could cultivate the land on your properties and give people work," I said, my confusion and his long speeches having provoked this flippant outburst.

"I have men who take care of that. What do you say?"

I looked at the pool and imagined Luke in it. "Well, I don't know, Eduardo. I'll have to ask my wife."

"Good." He stood up to take in the lovely view of the sierra, with the peak of Benicadell silhouetted against the sky. "The two year stipulation is in case of unforeseen circumstances, by the way. I'm sure you'll be able to stay here for at least four, if not more."

"Oh, and what's the rent?"

"Half of what you pay now."

"Three hundred?" I blurted out.

"Exactly. In return, as I say, you must keep the place tidy, so that it is in good condition when you leave."

"I guess you'll want a deposit?" I asked, still in a state of shock.

"What for? I trust you. We can make a contract if you like, but my word is my word. Your policeman friend will tell you that, though he likes to joke with me. There is plenty of furniture in the house for yourselves and guests. If you wish to use the fourth bedroom, I will send my men with more furniture."

"No, no," I said, fearing that Emma's parents and mine might descend at the same time.

He looked at his Rolex. "I must go. Here are two sets of keys."

"But I'll have to ask my wife first."

"If she says no, give the keys to Álvaro. I will call in to see you in a couple of weeks. Hasta luego, Sam."

"Hasta luego… y gracias."


Before going home I drove up to Álvaro's casita and told him the news. He laughed and patted me on the shoulder, making me wonder if he too were one of Eduardo's men.

"Ha, the scoundrel loves to act in such a dramatic way!"

"But is he a scoundrel? (Sinvergüenza in Spanish, by the way, a much-used word.) I can't take Emma and Luke there and then find that he changes his mind, can I?"

"He won't. I think his idea is a very prudent one. Now everyone is trying to sell, including my two colleagues, so prices are dropping at an alarming rate. Neither of them will be retiring for a long time," he said with a shake of the head. "Poor men, it pains me to see them so sad. They shouldn't have been so greedy."

"They didn't have Chelo to advise them."

"So, will you accept his offer?"

"I would, but it's up to Emma, and Luke too, I guess. I don't know if it'd mean him changing school."

"Why?"

"Well, don't you have to use a school near where you live?"

"Technically, yes, but who is to know?"

"Well, the address…"

"Pah! Then you don't tell them you have moved. This is Spain, Sam. This house, for instance, doesn't exist, so I don't pay the municipal tax," he said proudly. "Now, off you go to tell Emma."

"I don't know what she'll say."

"This weekend I will help you to move house."

"What?" said Emma, so I told her the story, omitting nothing.

"So you think Luke would be able to stay at the same school?"

"Emma, this is Spain. Folk don't worry about such minor details here. We'll keep the same post office box anyway," I said, having thought of that on the drive back.

"It sounds too good to be true."

"Well, it's about time we had a bit of luck, and the views are great down there. We'll be able to swim in the pool and look at the mountains."

"Hmm, and I suppose it's only a fifteen minute drive from Albaida."

"Call it twenty, as the house is a couple of miles past it, but it'll be worth it."

Luke was inside watching a cartoon, so we went in to break the news.

"I don't want to move. I like it here. I like playing with Oscar and Claudia. I like my school," he said, his uncompromising tone reminding me of his mother.

"You won't have to change school, and we'll have a swimming pool," said Emma.

"When do we go?" he asked, bouncing off the sofa.

I looked at Emma.

"Soon, love."

# 16

So we moved, not that weekend but the next, losing ten days' rent with carefree abandon. The fact that many Spanish rental properties are furnished is a great boon to flexibility, if you're not too fussy about that sort of thing, and as the furniture that Eduardo had moved from his Pou Clar property was quality stuff, we were more than happy with our roomy new residence, which would have an internet connection within a fortnight. Álvaro proved to know a lot about pools for a man who didn't have one, and after a bit of tinkering, cleaning, hoovering, and great quantities of noxious liquids, the pump was soon chugging away and within a day the water was Caribbean blue, thanks to the tiles, of course.

"It feels like being on holiday," I said that Sunday evening.

"It won't tomorrow, not for me anyway, though it'll be great to get back here and have a dip," said Emma, her hair still wet from her first swim.

"This time last year I was working my fingers to the bone."

"Yes, and we've still got a bank balance to prove it." She ruffled my hair, which was also wet, as had Luke's been until we'd finally coaxed him out of the pool, fed him, and put him to bed. The water was still quite cold, but we Yorkshire folk are tough and can put up with all kinds of hardship.

"We've got almond and olive trees," I said, not wishing to broach the subjects of work and money just then. "Though Eduardo might have men to see to them."

(This proved to be true, as a few weeks later a man on a tractor came to plough the acre or so of land.)

"It makes me feel more optimistic being here," said Emma. "I'm sure things'll get better for you now; not like before, but you were overdoing it anyway."

"Yep, I feel kinda lucky," I said, before going to open the bottle of cava that had just happened to be in the fridge which had just happened to be switched on when we arrived. Good old Eduardo, I thought as the cork hit the ceiling.

Our honeymoon period at the new house lasted until about the end of July, for me at least. I did a few minor jobs, mostly thanks to my flyer campaign, and I was glad that I was working on one of them when my parents came out at the end of June. Emma and I had agreed to say that things were looking up, and to back this up we omitted to tell them that the rent was so cheap.

"It's not like before, but I keep busy," I told them on arriving home from work, suitably soiled and sweaty.

"I'm pretty busy too," Emma told them.

"It's brilliant here," Luke told them.

"Mm, maybe you should stay on for a bit longer," my dad said from his floating li-lo.

"Yes, it looks like a good life to me," said my mum from her chair in the shade.

We conversed much more during the week, of course, but that's all you need to know. Emma's parents came out a fortnight later and I'd saved my last job, a small terrace roof at a house near the village of Benimarfull, for their visit, though I started work early and knocked off at about two each day.

"I *knew* things would turn out all right," said Cathy from the same li-lo my dad had used. "Oh, what a life! Wouldn't you prefer this, Dan?"

"It's fine for a holiday," Emma's dad said from the shade of the porch, glass of beer in hand. "But I'd have nowt to do here, and nor would you."

"Oh, we'd find things to do," said she.

"We've *got* things to do," said he. "We lead full lives. We've got our interests and lots of friends who share them. You don't change all that for a bit of sun."

"A *bit* of sun, he says!" Cathy shrieked, before rolling into the water.

In August the work dried up as inland Spain went to sleep for a month, but Emma was having a well-earned rest and I kept any gloomy thoughts to myself. We'd thought about driving up to the north of Spain to get out of the heat for a week or two, but due to my prospects I didn't wish to spend too much of our savings. I normally went cycling at first light, and a couple of hours on the bike helped to keep my spirits up for the rest of the day.

Having the pool, we found that Álvaro and Chelo visited more often, as did a couple of Emma's pals, and one of Luke's school-friends whose father was, believe it or not, a builder. When he came to pick up his son Pablo one day I invited him to a beer.

"What are your prospects like now?" I asked the wiry man who was also called Pablo.

"Zero. I was working for a big firm in Alzira, but that's over. We were building a housing estate for foreigners and one day the boss came round and told us all to go home. I drove past the other week to see if he'd kept anyone on. The cranes were still there, but there wasn't a soul around."

"What are you planning to do?"

"Claim the dole, of course. I'll get that for two years and as we've got two kids it's pretty good, almost 70% of my wage, in fact. We'll manage, and by the time it finishes things should have improved."

"So are you not thinking of setting up on your own or anything?"

"What's the point? There's no work out there now. No, I'll bide my time. I'm glad of the rest. No beach for us this year, but we've got my wife's parents' casita to go to," he said with a smile and a shrug.

This conversation cheered me up rather than otherwise, as if most Spanish building workers took the same laissez-faire attitude as Pablo Sr., and many foreign so-called builders went home, what little work there was would be more likely to come my way. Emma agreed and thought that when people came to accept the fact that their properties were going to lose value they might carry on as normal.

"What goes down usually comes back up, so the folk who are sticking around will calm down after a while and hopefully get any work done that they'd planned to do before all the bad news scared them. Yes, you might find that after the summer things will improve. It's the builders who weather the storm who'll get the work, so let's hope a really good job comes up soon."

During the first week in September no matter how often I checked my phone it still didn't ring. Then, like buses, I received three calls within a short space of time.

The first was from a Dane who had bought an old house in Alfafara and wanted a quote for doing it up from top to bottom.

The second was from Darren, telling me he had a big job in Tavernes de la Valldigna, near to his home. A German had bought a tumbledown house and wanted it doing up from top to bottom. I told him about my Danish caller's uncannily similar request and said I'd get back to him.

The third was from Barry, telling me that he urgently needed his third, unused, bedroom tiling, plastering and painting. I told him about the first two calls and he decided that he wasn't in such a hurry after all. He'd visited our new house, by the way, and had proven to be a strong swimmer for his age, due, he said, to his regular trips to the pool in Rafol de Salem. It's wonderful how even the smallest villages in Spain have municipal pools, but this is no time to digress.

The Dane was a big man in his fifties and looked like a Viking whose longship had washed up on a Caribbean island. His skin was of a purply-brown hue and his greying blond hair lapped over his broad shoulders. His name was Jonas and he lived near Jávea. He'd bought the old house as an investment some time ago and had decided to do it up.

"Is now the right time?" I asked, foolishly.

"Now I hope to find a builder who will do it for a reasonable price," he said in his near-perfect English.

"Right," I said, having resolved to say nothing else to dissuade him. "I'll have a look round and give you an approximate quote now, if you like."

"Go ahead. I wish the materials to be of average quality because I intend to rent or sell the house."

Who to? I thought. Did these Northern Europeans know something we didn't? Just when loads of Brits were talking about leaving, this man intended to set about coolly investing his money in a house that would soon sell for peanuts or have to compete in a rapidly growing rental market. Like Emma, however, he proved to be a mind-reader.

"Ha, you think I'm mad, but that is not so."

"Of course not."

"One must think in the long term and not pay attention to fluctuations. The house is mine and the cost of renovating it will not vary so much, so why not do it now?"

"Of course."

"Though I hope you will do better than the builders who came to see the house last year. Their quotes were ridiculous. Please proceed," he said, before lighting a small cigar and stepping out onto the steep street.

The house had three narrow storeys, each one more neglected than the last. It seemed structurally undamaged and I was relieved to see that the roof beams were sound, as was the roof, because setting up scaffolding on such an incline was a job for the experts. There was much to do, however, and I was reluctant to give him a quote that I might later regret, like the one I gave Brian for his luxury woodshed. Instead, I told him I'd prefer to charge him as we went along.

"Hmm, but I don't want to be travelling up from the coast too often," he said, his blue eyes gazing into my ever so trustworthy brown ones. "What would you do first?"

"I'd start on the top floor. I'd remove the plaster and the tiles and, er, plaster the walls and ceilings, and lay new tiles."

"What about the windows and doors?"

"I'd sand and varnish the doors, as they're nice old ones, but I think I'd change the windows… for some with brown PVC frames," I said, feeling like I was taking an oral examination.

"Good. Please call me with an exact quote for the top floor. If I agree you can get the key from the neighbour at number five – he's called Pepe, of course – and begin."

"Right, I'll go and take measurements."

While I was measuring and taking notes a thought crossed my mind, which I formulated into words on my way down the stairs.

"Pepe will have some money for you," he said before I could open my mouth. He stepped out onto the street and prepared to lock the door.

"What about colours?" I asked.

"Terracotta tiles and brown window frames. We will speak about painting later." He handed me a card. "Goodbye for now, Sam."

As I drove back down the sinuous road into Ontinyent I felt like I had the whole job in the bag. I was sure that in the heady days of prosperity the quotes he'd received would have been sky-high, so by limiting my projected net earnings to about fifteen euros an hour I was confident that he'd give me the go-ahead. I called in at the builders' merchant to check prices and before Emma and Luke arrived home I'd done my calculations and called Jonah. He assured me that providing my subsequent quotes for the rest of the house were similarly realistic, the work was mine.

On the short walk from her car to the porch I filled Emma in about the events of the day.

"That's brilliant, but calm down, love."

"Dad's excited," said Luke, who'd only recently stopped calling me daddy, as he'd now reached the mature age of eight.

"Darren's got an even bigger job down his way. I might see if I can do two or three days a week for him and–"

"Stop right there," said Emma, showing me the flat of her hand. "You are *not* going to end up working six or seven days a week like before."

"No, but–"

"No buts. You do your job and let Darren do his. You'll both be keeping your eyes open for other work, so I'm sure you'll get the chance to work together again, and if this Danish chap isn't in a hurry, why not work just four days a week? Make it last. You're blooming murder when you're not working."

"Am I?"

"Yes, I know you try to hide it, but your gloominess permeates the whole house. So, four days a week and no more worries for a while," she said, before tweaking my nose and giving me a kiss. "Theresa and Geoff have sold their house."

"Have they? How much for?"

"I don't know, but she seemed relieved today. We'll miss her, but I think they've done the right thing. If you haven't got peace of mind, what have you got?"

"Tell me about it."

So that was the autumn and early winter taken care of. I was happy working on the Dane's house, four and occasionally five days a week, Emma seemed content enough with her classes and interpreting work, and Luke was as delighted as ever at school. I've realised that I haven't written much about my son, not because I don't adore him, but because he was such an even-tempered, placid kid that our ups and downs never seemed to affect him. He appeared to have acquired the insouciance of most Spanish children, and many adults, and just took things in his stride.

I think now's the time to move things on a little, as you probably don't want to hear about our third Christmas holiday in Yorkshire. Our relationships with our families and friends remained constant and we were fairly happy most of the time, but my work prospects always lay lurking in the back of my mind, coming to the fore towards the end of each job. After a quiet January, Darren landed a huge job near Denia. Huge for us, that is, as by then doing up a house seemed to be the pinnacle of our aspirations. This, however, was a biggie.

"We've got a house to do up, Sam," he told me on the phone.

"Another? That's good. Do you need me?"

"Yes, I need you to help me put the finishing touches to it," he said with a chuckle.

"What's it like?"

"Very grey."

"Meaning?"

"There's just a concrete frame."

"Nothing else?"

"Nope. That's as far as the last owners got. A Belgian's bought it and wants it finished by the summer."

"How big is it?" I asked, the nature of the job having yet to sink in.

"A bungalow. Three bedrooms, two bathrooms. Good money."

"Can we do that?" I asked, as after so long spent doing what amounted to little more than DIY work, it felt like he was asking me to build a stately home from scratch.

"Ha we are builders, aren't we? I'll get a labourer too, and maybe some other men as and when. I'll not struggle to find them. Of course, if you're busy…"

"Well, I've a got a fence to paint."

"God, that sounds like something out of Tom Sawyer. Tell them to get a bloody painter."

"I will. When do we start?"

"Tomorrow."

# 17

Four months flashed by and I was back where I'd started. If that sounds ungrateful, cynical, or just plain lazy, I'm sorry, but that's the way it was. For the first two months, as we laid blocks, bricks and tiles, it was like old times. I'd get home each evening tired but content and look forward to the weekend with my family. As soon as the end was in sight, however, I started to worry again. A week or two off, fine, but what then? This Belgian build was a flash in the pan, we knew, and after that it'd be back to scratting around for work like Boy Scouts on Bob a Job day.

"We're almost done in Denia now," I said one Friday evening in June. "Another week or two, and that'll be it."

"Well, it's been great while it's lasted. It almost felt like being back in England again," said Emma from her horizontal positon on the leather sofa.

"Yes, it did, but it doesn't now. Now it's back to crappy jobs again, and probably a two-month summer holiday that I don't want. It's all right for you, love. You've got steady work all year round, but I'm sick of these bloody ups and downs."

"Excuse me?" she said, very ominously indeed. When she sat up and glared at me I knew I'd said something wrong and I had an inkling what it was.

.

"Er, I mean, well, it's better to have steady work, isn't it?"

"Sam, I'm a primary school teacher."

"Yes, I know."

"I'm a primary school teacher who is now teaching Spanish to mostly old people who have time to kill. I teach English to a couple of dull teenagers whose parents want them to pass their exams. I go with people to the doctor's and translate their ailments, or to the police station to help them to sort out their documents. Is that an ideal life for a primary school teacher?" she said, pausing between each sentence to allow the information to penetrate my dense skull and reach the tiny brain within.

"No, but you've never complained about it before."

"I don't mind doing it, but it's not and never will be my proper work. And why complain? That would make two of us moping around the house, like you'll be doing soon."

"Why didn't you tell me this before?"

"Because there was nothing to tell. It's the sacrifice I've had to make in exchange for living here. Oh, it's all right, don't get me wrong, but I miss teaching and I miss belonging to a school. It's great to see the kids pass from year to year, getting bigger and sometimes brighter all the time. Ha, you look like you've seen a ghost!"

"The ghost of a schoolteacher? No, I'm just a bit taken aback. I guess we should just both accept that our work won't be as satisfying over here."

"Or start thinking about going back."

"Do you want to?"

"I don't know, but I want us to think about it seriously. I want us to weigh up the pros and cons and decide if we wouldn't be better off back in Yorkshire. There's no hurry, but six months from now I'd need to think about applying for jobs so that I could go back to work in September next year." She came over and sat on the arm of my chair. "Now we've got the summer to enjoy, but come the autumn we'll have to see how things develop."

"What about teaching kids at the language school?"

"I've thought about that, but I'd never see you during the week, and little enough of Luke. No, it's a non-starter."

"Would we go back to Todmorden?"

"I think so. I've thought about that too. I wouldn't be able to get a job in the town right away, of course, but if we settled down somewhere else you'd have to start from scratch. In Tod you'd get some work pretty quick and you'd soon build it up again. You've got a reputation there, but in a new place there'll be plenty of established builders to compete with, and things aren't great in England now either. Do you fancy a beer?"

"Please," I said, still a bit stunned, especially by Emma's revelation about the unsatisfactory nature of her work. I guess I'd been thinking about myself too much and just assumed that when she drove off with her briefcase she was going to spend the day in a highly rewarding way.

"Let's put it to the back of our minds for now though," she said a while later as we drank our beer. "I don't want us to feel that we're in a sort of limbo. As things stand, we're staying, but at the beginning of 2011 we'll review the situation."

"OK, love."


So, we'd tacitly agreed not to talk about it, but that didn't stop me thinking about it on an almost daily basis. It seemed clear to me that in her heart of hearts Emma really wanted to go back and resume her teaching career, and who was I to stand in her way? I told Darren about our conversation as we were putting the finishing touches to the Belgian's fine chalet.

He wiped the dust from his hands. "Go back home then."

"Thanks, mate. I thought you enjoyed working with me?"

"Ha, I do, but after what you've said I think you might be best to give it a go back there."

"What, and if we don't like it come back here? I'd feel like a bloody yoyo."

"When you both get back into your work there you'll not want to come back, not for a long time anyway. Neither of you are the type who drifts along through life," he said, though he'd only met Emma once, at our new house the previous summer.

"Would you ever go back, Darren?"

"I don't think so, not unless one of us got ill or something. I'll be fifty-eight next month, so it'll soon be time to ease off the work a bit, though I'll not retire till I have to. Sheila likes the sun too much anyway."

"Hmm, I guess that's a big factor. Emma and me aren't exactly sun-worshippers. I mean, with the pool handy I can enjoy it for a while, but in summer I generally prefer the shade."

"Yes, we get enough sun at work."

"How are you fixed for... er, pensions?" I asked, hoping I wasn't prying too much.

"Not bad. We'll both get at least two-thirds of a state pension from back home if we pay more in towards the end. I'll get something from the Spanish state, but it's my private pensions that I'm counting on. I won't get much from my English one, but I've been paying a hell of a lot into my Spanish one for the last twelve years."

"Hmm, I guess that's what we'd need to do if we stayed."

"Starting right now."

"Yes, now, when there's hardly any work," I said, looking at the finished house and wishing it had been twice the size.

"You came out at an awkward time really, sort of half way through your working lives. Then there's this bloody crash. I've had twelve good years and one bad one, but we'll never see another building boom like that one here again."

"Never?"

"Never. It was crazy. Every bloody town's got blocks of empty flats and streets of unfinished houses that no-one needs." He shook his head. "I'll be all right, but you've got the next twenty years to think about."

"Yes, maybe we should go back."

"Go back and come out on holiday. Then you can say, 'Ooh, isn't it great living here. Aren't you lucky?' and stuff like that."

"Ha, yes, we could do that," I said, doing a rapid review of the people we could visit. Álvaro for sure, and Barry too, plus a couple of people Emma knew, but not, God forbid, Brian of the Woodshed.

"You'd be more than welcome to stay at ours for a week or so, you know. You could wave to me from the pool when I get home from work."

"Ha, that rings a bell! Yes, we'd definitely do that. Thanks, Darren."

"It'd be my pleasure. I'll just go and see how the electricians are getting on."

Once the seed of an idea is planted, it grows whether you like it or not. On the whole, however, I found it made the very quiet summer months more bearable, as having a Plan B made my enforced idleness less onerous. I got some small jobs and even tiled the floor of a small flat in August, where the air conditioning made the work quite pleasant, but most of the time I cycled, swam and performed household chores. We didn't go back to Yorkshire, and not just because of the expensive flights. We both knew that the subject of our possible return would come up and neither of us wanted to be influenced by our folks. Luke as yet knew nothing of

Plan B, because we knew that leaving his friends and returning to school in England would be traumatic for him, so why worry him if it might not even happen?

I didn't mention our dilemma to Álvaro until September, and then only because Chelo happened to be at his casita when I called. Álvaro tended to make off the cuff remarks which, though amusing, weren't always helpful, so I seized the opportunity of broaching the subject in the presence of his more objective partner.

Che, Sam, you can't go back," was his response to my initial comments, just as I'd expected.

"Why not?"

"Well, you can't throw in the towel so soon. Between the two of you, you can make enough money to get by, so why go back to that miserable island?"

"Have you ever been there, Álvaro?"

"No, but it must be awful, or why do so many of you come here?"

"It's lovely there," said Chelo. "I once visited the Cotswolds. Such pretty green countryside."

"Yes, it's not bad where I come from either. What do you think, Chelo?"

"Well, maybe because of my work I always tend to look at things from a financial point of view," she said, looking at me as if she thought this might not be helpful.

"Go on."

"From that point of view, I would advise you to go back. Spain is facing a terrible time now, and I don't think you are the kind of people who just want to get by," she said with a meaningful glance at Álvaro.

"That's what Darren, my building colleague, said."

Chelo went on to appraise our financial prospects and the subject of pensions reared its ugly head. "Estáis en tierra de nadie," she concluded, which as you might know or guess, meant that we were in no-man's-land.

"I know, we say that too."

"You must come to visit," Álvaro said, capitulating remarkably quickly in the face of Chelo's stark financial forecast.

"Oh, we will, don't worry about that."


The following month I was forced to acquiesce to Barry's insistent demands regarding his spare room renovation.

"You'd be best to go back," he said over our afternoon glass of wine.

"Everyone seems to be trying to get rid of us."

"Well they must have your best interests at heart. I mean, all things considered it's a no-brainer. You've given it your best shot and you have to think about Emma too. I mean, I just made parts for aeroplane engines, but I loved it, so school-teaching must be something special if you've got a vocation for it. Anyway, why do you think I've got you to do that bedroom up?"

"I've often wondered."

"For you to stay in, of course... or Luke, and you can have the other spare one."

"Is that true?"

"Well, partly. I've seen this coming for some time, but I don't want to lose sight of you altogether. This country's all right for an old bugger like me, but it's no place to get ahead in. Go back and teach and build things worth building," he said, motioning towards the sky, presumably indicating the plane which would transport us back to our productive lives.

So, as the autumn progressed, Plan B turned imperceptibly into Plan A. Emma and I couldn't avoid discussing it, of course, and it appeared that she'd received similarly sound advice from her friends Caroline and Jane, among other people. Jane's husband, Brian of the Woodshed, however, thought it a cowardly move, but I expected no less of the cretinous buffoon, and I shan't insult him anymore, unless I get the chance.

"So, I guess if you get a job for next September we could leave in the summer," I said one evening after Luke had gone to bed.

"Ye-es."

"You sound doubtful."

"Well, don't you think that once the ball's rolling we ought to go back sooner rather than later?"

"Maybe."

"The sooner we go back, the sooner you'll start getting work. I'm sure I'll get some supply work until a job comes up."

"Hmm." I closed my eyes and pictured the English winter, before also imagining the months of odd jobs that lay ahead of me, time that might be better spent touting for trade back in Tod. "When then?"

"How about in the New Year? I'd rather it was in the school holidays, you see, so that it won't be so bad for Luke. He could spend the rest of the school year adapting to the syllabus there. I think if I give him a bit of extra tuition he should be up to speed by the summer, as the standard's pretty high here."

"I'd better call Eduardo then. Oh, and when you're in town tomorrow, could you do me a favour?"

"What?"

"Take me off the damn autónomos once and for all."

"Ha, I'll do that."

The next day I told Eduardo that we were off at the end of the year and that we'd leave his house spick and span.

"That's a shame, Sam, but I think it is the right decision. This country is sinking into a bottomless pit."

"How are you getting on?"

"It is fortunate that I amassed a good deal of money in the good years. I am biding my time and holding on to my properties."

"Will you find someone to look after this place?"

"Oh, yes, I have a man who will take care of it."

"Of course."

When we broke the news to Luke he wasn't impressed. He cried, in fact, and was inconsolable for about an hour, after which he emerged from his room and asked when he'd be able to visit his friends.

"Maybe at Easter, but definitely in the summer. In the summer we're going to come back for a month," his mum said, stroking his hair and preparing for a fresh outburst of grief.

"That's all right then. And can Pablo visit us?"

"Whenever he wants."

"Where will we live?"

"Er, we're still thinking about that, love."

We were still thinking about that because my father's reaction to our news wasn't a practical one.

"Right, good. Well, I'll go round to your house tomorrow and tell them to pack their bags."

"Dad, it doesn't work like that. They have a contract until next July and even then it might not be easy to get them out. Besides, they're great tenants, as you've seen."

"Ay, the place is always shipshape when I go snooping round. You'll have to come here then."

This option had been in the back of our minds, but neither Emma nor I considered it ideal, though Luke thought it might be fun for a while. Their house was a spacious semi with big gardens, typical of those built in the 1960s when space wasn't at such a premium, but though we'd have our own bedrooms, we'd have to share the living area with my folks. Emma's parents' house wasn't an option as their third bedroom had long been converted into a study, housing a multitude of books and files appertaining to their respective hobbies.

"We'll see, Dad, and thanks for the offer."

"Back for Christmas then?"

"No, we've decided to spend our last Christmas here, to say goodbye to folk, you know."

"Ay, well, just let us know when you're coming. Shall I put your mother on?"

"Not now, Dad. Tell her I'll call again soon."

# 18

On the fourth of January 2011 we were residents of the United Kingdom once more. After a sociable Christmas spent visiting Barry, Darren, Álvaro and Chelo, and Emma's friend Caroline, we travelled back with a single suitcase each, having entrusted the rest of our stuff to a removal firm that was doing a brisk trade, mostly from Spain to Britain. It was cool and sunny when we left Alicante and cold, windy and raining when we arrived at Leeds-Bradford airport.

"Just what I expected," Emma said happily as we hurried over to the terminal building.

"I won't be able to work till April. I'm not acclimatised and my fingers would drop off," I said, though I knew my Dad had already lined up a little something for me in the way of work, indoors too, thank goodness.

Dan and Cathy picked us up and drove us straight to Todmorden, as Luke had to start school in two days' time. As we sat in the back of their Ford Focus I could see Cathy eying me in the mirror, so I smiled sweetly.

"Are you sad about coming back, Sam?" she asked in appropriately dulcet tones.

"Funnily enough I'm not, no. We'd just have been killing time if we'd stayed any longer. I'm looking forward to finding work and building up my business again."

"That's the spirit," she said, turning to smile at me as if I were putting a brave face on things, though what I'd said was quite true.

"Any work lined up, love?" Dan asked his daughter.

"Not yet, but they've said things will come up this term. Hopefully by September I'll have a permanent job somewhere not too far away."

"Back to school, back to school," said Luke in a singsong voice. We'd got him back into his old school, where he would spend a year and a half before going to secondary school. Three and a half years was a long time away, but we hoped he'd soon reacquaint himself with his friends, though he seemed less worried about it than we were.

"Now then," said my dad on our arrival, which was his way of greeting me after seven months apart. "Your stuff's arrived and your rooms are ready."

"Cup of tea?" my mum asked.

After a quick cuppa, Cathy and Dan headed back to Sowerby Bridge and we went upstairs to arrange our possessions as best we could.

"It'll be strange living here," said Emma as she filled a drawer.

"Yes, hopefully it won't be for too long, and at least it's cheap, well, free."

"Aren't we lucky that we've got family to look after us?"

"Yes, but I'm glad I'm not in the other bedroom. It'd make me feel like I was a kid again."

Luke came bursting in. "I'm going to play out for a bit."

"Mind the roads. Remember that the traffic comes the other way, and put your big coat on," said Emma.

"Will do," he said, though he didn't, but he came back an hour later, red-faced and boiling hot. England's not the North Pole, after all, and he got used to the winter weather faster than we did. De-icing my dad's car was probably the most annoying aspect of our first weeks back, that and de-icing the second-hand van that I soon bought.

One unexpected joy was the ease with which I became self-employed again. After an hour on the laptop I shut the lid and turned to Emma.

"That's it, done. I can't believe it. Why couldn't it have been so easy in Spain?"

"Because they don't do things that way. Besides, I think most people enjoy going to the gestoría. It's just another excuse to chat."

"I'd rather not chat about tax. You know, I only have to pay about forty quid a month N.I. contributions at first. It's as if they don't want people to set up small businesses in Spain."

"They'll catch up eventually. Maybe they'll change things now, to try to revitalise the economy."

"I bet they don't." (They haven't, though I believe autónomos is a bit cheaper for the first few months now.)

"Your dad's plotting something to do with our house."

"Is he?"

"Yes, he had that plotting look on his face."

"Oh, we'll manage here till the summer. I'm sure the tenants'll go then."

"I popped round to your house the other day," my dad said over dinner, a delicious home-made steak and kidney pie, chips and veg.

"You should've left that to me, Dad."

"Ay, well, I was passing. Anyway, nothing to worry about there. They're leaving in April."

"What? Why?" I asked, my suspicions aroused, as the last time Emma had emailed the rental agency they'd had no plans to move. "You didn't threaten them, did you? Or write 'Southerners Go

Home' on the window?" Our tenants were originally from Coventry, which was the south as far as my father was concerned.

"No, we had a chat and it turns out they're thinking of buying a place."

"I'm going round there tomorrow."

"Suit yourself," he said, before spearing a carrot with great nonchalance.

I ended up calling on them at the weekend and the young couple told me rather sheepishly that my dad had offered them £2000 if they'd leave three months early.

"It suited us really, because we've got our eyes on a house and it'll help to pay for the furniture," the man said with imploring eyes. "I know it's a bit irregular, and we'll scrap the idea if you want."

"There's no need. My dad's a big lad and he can choose how to spend his money, if you're happy with the arrangement, that is. You can stay till July, you know."

"Oh, no, no…"

This seemingly irrelevant exchange went on for a bit longer before I took my leave, and I only mention it because it reminded me how polite us British folk can be. The Spanish are very brash, on the whole, and many of them would have been delighted to pocket the two grand, maybe feeling shrewd to have pulled a fast one. I generalise, of course, but it took me a while to get used to our gentle civility again. As I renewed old friendships and acquaintances I decided that, on the whole, I preferred the English people who live in England to those who live in Spain. For some Brits abroad, being an expat is their *raison d'être* and they talk about nothing else, so it was good to get back to nice, unassuming folk going about their daily business.

As I walked the streets of Todmorden, for I had a lot of spare time for the first month or so, I realised in a rather naïve way that there are tens of millions of people living in Britain who actually like it. When a pleasant lady in the bakery said that it was a shame that we'd had to come back, I asked her if she'd ever thought about emigrating.

"Me? What on earth for? That'll be two-forty, love."

By the time we moved back into our long-lost home I was working at least thirty hours a week and Emma was getting supply work almost all the time, which she drove to in the second-hand Fiat Panda that we picked up fairly cheaply. As for Luke, it was as if he'd never been away, though his form teacher did point out that he was rather too keen on showing off his Spanish. When we visited the local tapas bar, however, he began to speak to us in Valenciano, a sure sign that his adolescent years were just around the corner. In the last five years he's got plenty of mileage out of his language skills, which we've all brushed up on during our twice-yearly visits to see our friends, and we're still pretty proud to be able to speak it, some (me) worse than others.

"Do you feel that we're worse off because of our time in Spain?" I asked Emma a few days after we'd moved back into our house.

"What, monetarily?"

"Well, everything, really."

She churned the old grey matter around for a moment. "Well, financially we'd have been better off if we'd stayed, of course, but so what?"

"We might have bought a better house."

"What? A detached house about a yard away from the next one?"

"Well, yes, or maybe somewhere in the country."

"Hmm, I'd like that more. Anyway, apart from that I wouldn't change it for anything in the world. It's as if we've had another mini-life in Spain, and we can always go back one day."

"When we get our pensions?"

"Exactly, or when we're absolutely sure we're going to have enough to live on, but I don't want to think about that for a long, long time. We've got our lives to lead and when it rains there's no point pining for the sun."

"No, and it was bloody hot working out there in summer. You start to respect the sun when you're forced to be out in it."

"When I'm at work I couldn't care less what the weather's doing. I can't wait to get my own class again."

"Yes, I prefer working here too. I get more interesting jobs and, well, I feel more at home around the folk in the trade. Working abroad you feel like an outsider, even an interloper."

"Yes, I think Spain is ideal for leisure, but not for work. Can we afford to go out for a week at Easter?"

"Oh, I think we can scrape the money for the flights together. Dad'll have to wait a bit for his two grand back."

"It was his idea."

"To get us out from under his feet, but I'll pay him back, eventually."

# Postscript – October 2016

Five years' worth of water has run down the River Calder, so I'll tell you where we're up to now. Six months ago we moved into our new house, a large stone cottage in the countryside quite near to Todmorden. It cost us an arm and a leg, but as we're both doing well at work it shouldn't take us more than ten years to pay off the mortgage. I've never thought of Emma and I as go-getters, but I suppose we are in a way, and that has its rewards. Besides, I enjoy teaching my apprentice the skills of the trade, just like Walter taught me, and I might well keep him on when he qualifies.

We love it in the country and it's wonderful to be able to step out of the door straight onto a footpath up to the moors. We walk all year round and enjoy the changing of the seasons and the unpredictability of the weather. It's best when it's sunny, of course, but you appreciate it more when you don't have it all the time. I certainly don't miss the long, relentless Spanish summers, though I'd be fibbing if I said that I didn't sometimes yearn for those warm springs and autumns. Had we gone to live in Spain at a more opportune time, I'm sure I'd have carved out a good building career there, but I don't think Emma would ever have been satisfied with the kind of teaching work available to her.

After supply teaching up and down the valley for two years, she landed a job back in Tod, though at a different primary school. She's about to be promoted and I fully expect her to end up being the head of that or another school within the next few years, such is her ability and dedication to her profession. She's now doing a Spanish degree through the Open University, and Castellano is often spoken in our house, as even I can still string a decent sentence together. Luke intends to study it at university, along with French and maybe Italian, when he heads off into the big wide world about three years from now.

And Spain? Well, we always go out at Easter and in late summer, and while Luke spends most of his time at his pal Pablo's house, we do the rounds of our friends. (Pablo Sr. is a sales rep now, by the way. He's inordinately proud of his manicured nails, so he mustn't have had building in his blood like me.) Barry's over eighty now and still fighting fit. He has no intention of going back to England and if he should ever need looking after he says there are plenty of willing women in the village. He says that with a twinkle in his eye, as there's still life in the old dog yet, though his dog Figo died recently, so I put him on to Sophie and he's about to adopt one of the half dozen that live in the extension I built.

"You'll not get me back to England, duck," he said only a few weeks ago as we sat beside the local swimming pool.

"Ooh, it must be wonderful living here," I replied, something I also said down at Darren's whenever we spent a few days with him and Sheila. He'd soldiered on through the depression, never being without work for long, and was as good-humoured as ever.

"It's sod's law. Work's picking up again now just when I want to ease off."

"You could retire," said Sheila from her sunbed.

"Nah, not for another few years."

We spent most of our holiday time at Álvaro's, however, and I'm sure that he built his plunge pool at least partly with us in mind, as he rarely ventured into it. I quizzed him about this one day when Emma had gone to see Caroline and Jane. (Brian of the Woodshed is feeling happier now, by the way, as the value of his house is rising again, though his dodgy deeds still annoy him.)

"The pool for you? You must be joking. Why would I do that after you deserted us and went back to your miserable country? No, it's for the grandchildren," he said, as both his daughters now had two kids each.

"How's Eduardo, by the way?"

"I've seen more of him lately. I think the beast is beginning to stir."

"Give him my regards. When are you and Chelo coming to visit us?"

"Soon, soon," he said, though he's been saying that for five years now.

When Chelo was around I sometimes discussed pensions with her, sad as that may sound, for I'd developed an almost unhealthy interest in my private scheme, which I esteemed like a crock of gold under my bed. Our pension quandary had been a major factor in our decision to leave, that and Emma's work, and I often went online to see how mine was progressing.

"Looking at that *again*, you sad character," Emma said one evening when I was supposed to be writing this.

"Well, you never know if we'll want to go back to live in Spain again one day."

"Do you?"

"I don't know. I don't think so, really," I said, stroking her cheek.

"No, me neither. When we retire we could rent places for a month or two at a time. Then we could explore different parts of Spain."

"That's a good idea, and much less fuss than living there. Besides, I like it here."

"Me too." She ruffled my very slightly greying hair. "We've become Hispanophiles since we lived there, but that doesn't mean we have to up sticks again, does it?"

"No, and we've got our parents to look after," I said, though they're still in good health, apart from Dan's piles. "Being an expat isn't all it's cracked up to be, is it?"

"It is for some, but not for us. Tim and Sue are still enjoying it, aren't they?"

"I believe so."

"Ha, those wicked people who turned our heads! Still, I have no regrets. Have you, Sam?"

"None at all, but I'd rather have the best of both worlds."

## APPENDIX – Some post-Brexit Observations

Do you remember when early in the book I began to spout forth my opinions and Emma told me to put a sock in it and get on with the story? Well, although I did my best to obey her, I still have a few more things to say, so I thought I'd save them for a separate bit at the end, so as not to spoil the narrative flow, such as it is.

Now that our exit from the European Union has put the cat among the pigeons, I reiterate even more strongly my opinion that it's best to do what we did; to rent out your UK home and rent a place in Spain for at least a year, if not two, before buying a property. There are many reasons for doing this, and the possibility of being swindled is only one of them, though I'll address that issue first. Not only the Brians of this world, but even Spanish people have been known to buy properties in the countryside only to find that there are discrepancies in the deeds. Álvaro tells me that this occurs most often with respect to the land adjoining the house, rather than the land which the house sits upon, but it can still be a serious problem and has been known to end in lengthy and costly litigation, if it ends, as it can just drag on forever.

If it happens to Spaniards then, how can we prevent it from happening to us? First of all, by getting to know the town or village that you're living in or near. We were lucky enough to encounter Helen before we set foot in Ontinyent, but that's not always possible and if you're unlucky you might end up contracting the services of a wrong 'un. Pound for pound there are far more British crooks in Spain than Spanish ones. Mobility is a great advantage for wrongdoers and British estate agents and suchlike are far more likely to do a bunk than their Spanish counterparts. If a Spanish lawyer, for example, fiddles a foreigner, the locals get to know about it and it isn't likely to do his or her business any good, so you should always choose a well-established local lawyer/gestor/asesor to work with. How can you be sure about their reputation? By living in the town for a while and finding out.

In most towns of more than 10,000 inhabitants within thirty miles of the Spanish Mediterranean coast there's likely to be more than one British person working as an interpreter, often several. Some of these are great, some are clueless, and a few might lead you down the garden path, maybe by taking you to the estate agent of their choice who has a couple of dodgy properties to unload. When new to a foreign country we find an English voice reassuring, but beware. Only on the local grapevine can you find out who the good interpreters are. We were just plain lucky with Helen, though if we ever go back to live in another part of Spain I shall want to see any potential 'fixers', be they Spanish or British, face-to-face, before sussing out if they know their stuff and are to be trusted. This might mean drinking a few more beers around the bars than I would like, but it would be money well spent.

Is all this blindingly obvious? Well, let me put the case of the hypothetical Mr and Mrs X to you. Mr and Mrs X work for thirty or forty years in their respective jobs. They do their best to get ahead, they go to work even when they feel unwell, they put up with crap from time to time when they have a bad boss, if they lose their job they do their damnedest to get another one double-quick, as there's a mortgage to be paid. In short, they try not to put a foot wrong during several decades, at the end of which they have a nice home and plenty of money in the bank. Then they sell up and put themselves in the hands of people they don't know from Adam and buy a property in Spain.

I mean, it's just not sensible, is it? Even though renting is sniffed at by many people in our country, it's by far the best option when you go to live abroad, and not only because you might get diddled. When you go to live in a place, you begin to accumulate knowledge, but not before. The internet's a great tool, but you simply can't believe everything you read online. I mentioned that during our period of research Emma always weighed up the motives of the authors of the articles, forum posts, or whatever, but even this isn't really enough. You need to meet people face-to-face in order to weigh them up. Body language and facial expressions are very revealing and we've relied on our analysis of them since the beginning of humankind when deciding whether to trust someone or not.

Has that suddenly ended? You only have to consider all the internet fraud that's going on – and it's not only gormless folk who are being duped – to realise that using the worldwide web has its limitations, and gathering information in order to make massive life-choices is one of them. I admit that you can glean a lot of useful stuff from blogs, articles and expat forums these days, but they should only play a part in your research, *not* in your decisions.

Let's imagine now that you've ignored my sage advice and bought a house somewhere in Spain. Everything goes through smoothly and you're sitting pretty. It's fine, it's OK, but a few months after you've moved in you discover a town or village more to your liking a few miles down the road. In Spain – as everywhere else, I guess – adjacent towns can have very different characters. With no disrespect to Ontinyent and its fine citizens, the people in Albaida and other nearby villages are more laid-back and generally more sociable than the inhabitants of the capital of the valley. If you walk into a bar you're more likely to get chatting to someone in a smaller place than a larger one, though in a larger place there's usually more going on. It's horses for courses.

Bloody obvious again, I hear you say. Why is it then that when people move to a new town or city in Britain they look at the place through a microscope and analyse the best districts, the best schools, and so on, but folk buy a place in Spain on the basis of a subjective recommendation and a flying visit? Most places on or very near the Spanish coast are home to many foreigners, but when you go just a few miles further inland you'll find some towns and villages with a thriving expat community and others with just a few stray Brits and other Europeans. Some of us like one kind of scene and some like another. Those who wish to integrate more would be wise to settle in a less 'colonised' place, while those who crave the company of their countrymen ought to make sure there'll be plenty of them around. How do you find out for sure? By living there for a while and exploring the area.

Then there's the environment. I know a couple who bought a house in the village of Algueña in Alicante. They'd sussed everything out online and thought it was the place for them; small but not too small, close to wooded hills, less expensive than other nearby villages. They all but did the deal on Skype and over the internet, so when they went out and found that one of the biggest marble quarries in Europe was right on their doorstep, they assimilated that slight inconvenience and signed the papers that were placed under their noses.

Silly sods, what? Well, they'd run a successful business in England for many years, facing many difficult choices along the way, but they were just too damn *polite* to change their minds. Besides, their house didn't face the humungous quarry, and the fact that the Chinese owners worked it 24/7 didn't cause them too many sleepless night, despite the dynamite, not to mention the dust which travels many a mile before settling down on the unsuspecting olive trees. Would they have stayed there for more than a year if they'd been renting? Would they hell. The house is up for sale now, but the quarry's still there, though in a couple of decades there won't be any mountain left. This is an extreme example, of course, but you need to get to know your countryside. There aren't nearly as many footpaths in Spain, and less right to roam, so that lovely mountainside you've ogled on your trip out might not be as accessible as you think.

I think the point I'm trying to make in this little rant – which Emma was quite right in advising me to keep out of our story – is that otherwise sensible people just don't think straight when it comes to moving abroad. Rent and rent, don't sell and buy, at least at first.

What about Brexit?

All the more reason to rent rather than buy, but other than that I don't think it's anything to worry about. After all, many people emigrate to non-EU countries and seem to get on all right. The worst case scenario is that British people will have to make monthly or yearly payments in order to access the (brilliant) Spanish health service. Officially and unofficially, there must be about a million Brits living in Spain now, and the Spanish government can ill afford to drive us away. The Valencian regional government has already spoken out on the issue, and they're all for us sticking around, so I don't expect there to be any great waves in the coming years. Still, it's yet another reason to rent…

I rest my case and my fingers. Adiós y buena suerte.

17241156R00115

Printed in Poland
by Amazon Fulfillment
Poland Sp. z o.o., Wrocław